A Fighting Chance

BOOK 1

by
Joe Manno

*Read on!
You are a leader!
God Bless*

RTC ENTERTAINMENT INC
REACHING THE CHILDREN

A Fighting Chance

by Joe Manno
Published by

RTC ENTERTAINMENT INC
REACHING THE CHILDREN

© 2002 RTC Entertainment, Inc.
P.O. Box 609138
Orlando, Florida 32860-9138
www.rtcentertainment.com

Cover design by Bill Johnson
Illustrations by Cynthia Woodhouse

International Standard Book Number 0-9718501-1-9

Printed and Published in the United States of America
07 08 09 10 — 9 8 7 6 5 4

Contents

Adam

Kelly

Dominique

Billy

DJ

Jackie

Yuri

Josh

Chapter 1

How It All Began

Bright sunlight beamed through the window, lighting up the bedroom. An unmade bed displayed a plain colored pillow on one side and a cartoon designed pillow on the other. The toilet flushed at the same time the alarm clock went off.

A grown man, wearing Looney Toon pajamas, stepped out of the bathroom and glanced out the window to admire the beautiful morning sunlight. He shuffled his way through the room to silence the annoying alarm clock nestled between several cartoon characters on the nightstand.

Carefully removing his pajamas, he neatly folded them and placed them on the bed. Next to the pajamas lay his outfit for the day. He began to dress, putting on an extremely dorky-looking paisley shirt and a pair of gray sweatpants. Not only did the sweatpants not match, but they were pulled up so high that he looked

A Fighting Chance

like he was all legs. To top this outfit off, he added a black bow tie and put on his round, black-rimmed glasses that he had just picked up from their prim and proper place on the nightstand. He then combed several strands of hair across the top of his head, trying to cover up his enormous patch of baldness.

He looked in the mirror at his slightly protruding teeth and truly liked what he saw, saying aloud, "Joseph Gunner, you are one handsome young man."

Not only did he look very odd, but he sounded that way, too. His Steve Urkel-sounding voice fit the way he looked to the tee.

Joseph Gunner turned to pick up his briefcase and tripped over his shoe. He fell against the nightstand, knocking off the cartoon characters. As he fell he reached for a small lamp thinking it would be able to stop his fall, but pulled it off the nightstand and crashed to the ground, lamp and all. Joseph tried desperately to get himself up and got all tangled up in the lamp cord. Twisting and turning, trying to get untangled, he somehow freed himself from the mess and walked out of the room, heading for the front door.

"Okay, that wasn't so bad."

He then yelled out to his wife, who was somewhere in the house, to let her know he was leaving.

"I'm off to school. See you this evening."

"Okay, honey," she yelled back. He turned to the front door, thinking he had already opened it and ran face first into the door.

"Honey, are you all right?" his wife calmly called out, familiar with this sort of thing happening around their house.

"I'm fine, dear. Don't worry about me. It's gonna take more than this silly little door to stop me from getting to school today."

Joseph closed the door, straightened his glasses, and approached his 1962 Metropolitan—a car so small that if you were sitting in it, you'd be eye-to-eye with a squirrel. Joseph saw his neighbor, a spunky eighty-seven-year-old woman, enjoying her morning walk down the driveway to get her newspaper.

"Hello, Mrs. Maldinati," he said in his screechy, nerdy voice.

She looked up and smiled, giving him a wave.

"Have a nice day, Mrs. Maldinati!" Joseph added.

Before she could answer, Joseph tripped on his newspaper and body slammed onto his tin can of a car. Mrs. Maldinati didn't even ask if he was all right. She just shook her head, picked up her newspaper and turned and walked back to her house.

"I'm okay," Joseph said. "The newspaper is just a little wet. That's what caused the slipping and the falling."

He realized she wasn't listening and knew that she really didn't want to hear excuses for his clumsiness, which happened on a regular basis.

Joseph got into his car and tried to get it out of first gear. He jerked the car out of the parking spot, screeching and revving the engine before finally reaching second gear.

Arriving at the first stop sign, he saw a group of kids waiting for the bus. Joseph stalled and restarted the engine. The car chugged and screeched as he drove away, trying to shift into different gears. The kids watched in amazement as the little tin can junker took off down the street. The silence was broken as they looked at each other and began laughing at what they just saw.

Chapter 2

The Bus Stop

Ten kids were standing around waiting for the bus. All ten were eighth graders at Metro Middle School. Five of them, Adam, Kelly, Billy, DJ and Josh, along with three others, Yuri, Jackie and Dominique, would meet later at school, having no idea what awaited them in the future. The two groups really didn't know each other—or care to know each other—and were most unlikely to get together. It was hard to imagine them ever being best friends.

While waiting for the bus, Billy and DJ were throwing around a Nerf football and Kelly, the cheerleader type, was talking to her friends. From time to time, she glanced at Billy. DJ was a jock, but Billy was more the looker.

The other kids were playing pocket video games, but Adam, the genius, was sitting on the curb. Several opened books were around him as he buried himself in another. His note pad was right next to him to jot down notes as he read.

The bus pulled up, and all the kids made their way toward the door. Billy, DJ, Kelly and a few of the others walked in their own group. Josh gathered up all the loose paper and garbage that was left on the ground and threw it into the nearby trashcan. He couldn't stand to see the environment messed up in any way. Josh was a quiet kid. He just did his thing and minded his own business.

Sometimes the other kids threw trash on the ground purposely just to aggravate Josh and see what he would do. He always picked up the trash and disposed of it, shaking his head in disgust but never saying a word.

One of the kids passed by Adam and flicked him on the back of the head. "Hey, brainiac, put your laboratory away. The bus is here!"

Billy and DJ laughed, but Kelly was more sympathetic.

"Give him a break. At least he uses his brain," Kelly added, helping Adam pick up his books before they got on the bus. Billy and DJ felt a little uncomfortable about laughing at him, while Adam just smiled, thinking how great it was that someone, especially a girl, was giving him the time of day.

Their bus pulled into the long line of school busses unloading kids as the morning congestion filled the campus at Metro Middle School. Miss Ward, the school principal, exited the front door of the school to greet as many students as she could before the first bell rang. Miss Ward was in her mid-thirties and, for the most part, was very friendly and personable with the kids. You could tell by the way the kids responded to her that she was well-liked.

Three guys approached Miss Ward to say their good mornings. Yuri, the shortest of the three boys, just laughed as always and nodded his head as he walked by. He was one of those kids who constantly had a smile on his face and would laugh at anything you said to him. He found humor in everything and everyone. People enjoyed being around Yuri because he was always laughing.

The school's vice principal, Mrs. Rossenheimer, joined Miss Ward. Mrs. Rossenheimer was not the happiest of people. She was about sixty-years-old and had a broomstick type of attitude. Miss Ward greeted her, "Good morning, Mrs. Rossenheimer."

"It's okay; I wouldn't call it good."

From out of nowhere, Jackie ran up to catch a football pass from another kid.

"Jackie, heads up!" the kid yelled out.

Jackie caught the ball and stopped just short of hitting Miss Ward.

"Sorry, Miss Ward."

"That's all right, dear," Miss Ward said kindly. "Now let's put the football away and get inside."

"Yes, ma'am," Jackie respectively added.

Jackie could be a real tomboy at times, joining the guys in any sport. She was not only first pick, but usually the team captain, no matter what the event.

Dominique, singing as always, and a few of her friends were heading in the direction of Mrs. Rossenheimer and Miss Ward. As they passed by, Dominique hit some high notes that got their attention. Mrs. Rossenheimer commented on the talent of her singing.

"I'll tell you, that girl might talk your ear off, but she sure can sing like a bird!"

"That she can!" Miss Ward responded, then changed the subject.

"The school board is sending us a gentleman to help some of our overworked teachers, since we have had such a population increase here lately."

"Where will he be working?" Mrs. Rossenheimer curiously questioned.

"He will be assisting Mr. Edwards in gym class and taking the new third period study hall we had to form."

"We can use all the help we can get!" Mrs. Rossenheimer added.

On that note, the bell rang and the two ladies entered the school.

Chapter 3

Adam's Experiment

Ms. Sanders was an eighth grade science teacher who, at any given time, would let her students get up in front of the class and explain an experiment or invention they might've come up with. Of course, no one ever had one, except for Adam. He usually had one or two inventions a week.

Adam stood next to Ms. Sanders, who was about to turn the entire class over to him so he could explain his new invention. She gently addressed the class.

"Quiet, please. Thank you. Adam, as we all know, likes to invent things. He's very creative. However, he has never invented anything to this degree. Whether it works or not, please give him your attention while he explains his invention to us."

Several of the kids in the class snickered under their breath at Adam.

A Fighting Chance

"Thank you, Ms. Sanders," said Adam.

"Class, if you'll excuse me for a moment, I'll be right back," Ms. Sanders said. As she left the room, a wad of paper hit Adam in the head while he reached for a piece of chalk. Adam didn't let the childlike behavior bother him.

"Thanks," he added, referring to the wad of paper that just whacked him on the head. Adam continued, "This is an ordinary piece of chalk."

"No kidding!" one of his classmates responded.

Kelly, who was also in this class, answered the rude remark, "Give him a break. Listen, you might learn something."

"Ah, Kelly likes Adam," another classmate blurted out.

Kelly really didn't "like" Adam or anything, she just didn't like to see him picked on.

"Grow up!" she fired back.

Adam, happy that someone was on his side, reacted, "Yeah, grow up!" He smiled, looking at Kelly.

Kelly rolled her eyes at Adam, assuring him that she had no interest in him at all. It was just a nice gesture in his defense. Adam continued as he once again focused on explaining his invention to the class.

"Every day we deal with the task of continually erasing this constructed piece of slate. Worry no more. I need three volunteers to write their names on the board."

Several hands went up, but most of the kids were

not even paying attention. Adam chose three people and directed them to the chalkboard.

"With your piece of chalk, write your first and last name on the board."

As the volunteers were writing, one of the kids in the class blurted out a put-down to one of the girls chosen to write on the board.

"How do you spell Lindsey?"

Lindsey turned and gave him a ridiculous look. Adam ignored both of them and kept talking.

"I've put together this box which transmits a high frequency of sound, that once it is pinpointed on an element, creates a diffusion of its molecules, causing breakdown immediately. However—"

Adam was interrupted by a classmate. "English. Give it to us in English, Brainiac."

Adam did not respond to the kid's remark, but realized that he was with eighth graders and not professors. He continued, keeping his explanation at their level.

"However, built into the front part of the box is a laser sensor that is used to pinpoint which molecules are targeted for destruction. For example, let me show you."

Adam began to demonstrate to the class.

"Let's say you wanted to erase just a portion of the board, like Lindsey's first name only. Point the laser at the desired area and drag it over that amount, just as you would if you were using a computer mouse. Once

A Fighting Chance

you have scanned over the section desired, you hit this little red button. Anyone want to try?"

Kelly raised her hand. She didn't wait for Adam to call on her. She got up and headed toward him with her eyes fixed on that little red button.

"I'll do it," she said with determination.

"Cool. Just push here whenever you are ready."

Kelly got all cutesy and pushed the red button. She didn't know or really care what was going to happen. She just wanted to get up in front of the class and participate in something that would draw attention to her. When she pushed the button, all attention was off of her as Lindsey's name powdered like granules of sugar and fell to the bottom ledge of the chalkboard. Silence fell over the class, for no one expected this to work.

Kelly broke the silence, "Cool!"

Another classmate responded, "Wow, that was great! Can you erase all of Lindsey?"

"Of course not, you can't dissolve people...yet." Adam knew what she meant, but he just liked playing with people's minds.

"No, I meant her entire name," she said.

Willing to show off more of his invention, Adam

proceeded confidently. "Sure it can. As a matter of fact, if you scan the laser on wide beam, you can erase the entire board at one time. Watch, let me show you."

Adam moved the knob to wide beam, setting the unit to do what he said it would do and then turned to Kelly, who had not gone back to her seat yet. After all, why should she? She'd get more attention if she just stood up there with Adam.

"Kelly, would you like to do the honors?"

Kelly just smiled in response and pushed the button. At the touch of the button, all the chalk on the board fell to the chalk catcher all at once.

A kid from the class called out. "Way to go, Brainiac. You finally did something that works."

Adam replied with confidence, "Everything I do works. I just don't show everything I do. Watch this." Adam pointed the laser at the kid who made the comment.

When the beam dot hit the kid's face, a panicked look flushed over him. The whole class looked startled.

"Just kidding," Adam said with a smirk.

The entire class began to rag on the kid because the so-called brainiac had him shaken.

Chapter 4

The School Meets Mr. Gunner

Joseph Gunner's tiny little car pulled into the parking lot and drove to the section marked for faculty. All the parking spots seemed to be taken, so Joseph circled around a few more times. There was a small space between the curb and the bike rack. Joseph stopped his car and took a look at the impossibly small space. No other car could ever dream of fitting in this spot! But this was no other car. This was a matchbox on steroids! Joseph shifted gears and safely glided into the spot.

Inside the principal's office, Miss Ward, Mrs. Rossenheimer and Mr. Edwards, the P.E. teacher, were discussing the arrival of the new teacher. Mr. Edwards had been teaching physical education for twenty years. He was a straightforward kind of guy and his personality was somewhat calm and easygoing. Miss Ward knew nothing about the new teacher, only what she had heard from the office of the Board of Education. She felt very confident in this teacher and encouraged Mr. Edwards.

"The Board sent his credentials and he seems to be a highly qualified educator."

"That sounds good to me," Mr. Edwards replied.

"I'm glad you approve," said Miss Ward, "because he'll be working right alongside of you."

Mr. Edwards was stunned. "You've got to be kidding!"

Miss Ward didn't understand why he would respond in such a negative way. "You've known about this for two days," she said.

Mr. Edwards didn't answer. He just stared through the office window and watched a strange man making his way toward their office. Miss Ward and Mrs. Rossenheimer locked in on the same stare. The man was Joseph Gunner and he had the entire office at a standstill. They were stunned to see what was walking in their presence. They did everything in their power to keep from laughing. It wasn't the man they were laughing at. It was his funny clothes and the way he walked that had them putting their hands over their mouths.

Josh, the young man who cared about the environment, was helping out in the office putting files away. He stopped in mid-action, staring at Joseph Gunner as he headed into the principal's office.

Mrs. Rossenheimer broke the silence. She just had

to speak out. "He's not your average-looking gym teacher. I mean, sweat pants, dress shoes, a paisley dress shirt and a bow tie?"

"You've got a point there," Miss Ward chuckled, but was just as confused.

Gunner knocked on the door.

"Come in," Miss Ward replied.

"We can hope that maybe he's not the gym teacher," Mr. Edwards commented.

Joseph Gunner entered the office loudly and clumsily.

"Good afternoon, my name is Joseph Gunner, the new physical education assistant. I believe you are expecting me?"

They all just wanted to pinch themselves and hope that this was a dream. However, Miss Ward answered respectfully.

"Yes, we are expecting you, Mr. Gunner. Welcome to Metro Middle School."

She introduced him to both Mrs. Rossenheimer and Mr. Edwards. Gunner extended his hand to shake theirs.

"It's a pleasure to meet both of you. I'm looking forward to working with you, Mr. Edwards. I'm sure we are going to have a great time working together, with the children and all."

Mr. Edwards gave a very respectful and distinguished smile.

"I'm sure it will be quite interesting," he replied.

Chapter 5

Gym Class

It was Joseph Gunner's first day on the job. It didn't take long for word to spread throughout the entire school.

Mr. Edwards gave Mr. Gunner an assignment to keep order in the boy's locker room while they dressed out for gym class. Trying to be firm in his Steve Urkel voice, he began to give orders.

"You boys need to get yourselves changed as quickly as possible and exit into the gym. Find yourself a seat on the floor in a most organized manner." At the same time he said "organized manner", a pair of boy's underwear landed on his head.

"I saw that, Mr. Allen," Gunner commented.

The entire locker room roared with laughter as Mr. Gunner walked into Mr. Edwards's office still wearing the underwear on his head. Mr. Edwards grinned slightly before addressing Gunner.

"You've got to keep an eye on those kids. They are very quick."

Always seeming to have a comeback, Gunner answered, "Yeah, well, they can't get anything past me, that's for sure. You've got to get up pretty early in the morning before you can pull a fast one on ol' Joseph Gunner!"

He said this with the confidence of a man who knew what he was talking about. He turned and walked proudly out of the office.

By then, Mr. Edwards was laughing, not only because of what Gunner just said, but because he saw a sign taped to Gunner's back that read "Mr. GunNERD."

Mr. Gunner walked back into the locker room, where a boy named Ben was still standing at his locker. Ben swiftly closed the locker door when he saw Mr. Gunner coming around the corner.

"You need to dress out a little more quickly from now on, Ben."

"Yes sir," a nervous Ben replied. He strolled, head down, into the gymnasium and sat in the middle of the other kids.

A dull roar began to fill the large room as everyone laughed at the hysterical sound of Gunner blowing his nose, which resembled the horn of a diesel truck.

The girls came in to join the boys waiting for class to start when Mr. Edwards returned from his office to give Gunner some last minute instructions.

"Gunner, can you get the kids warmed up? I've got some paperwork to do."

"No problem, Mr. Edwards. I can handle the job."

Mr. Edwards replied as he once again glanced at the sign on Gunner's back, "Be careful with these kids. Don't let them walk all over you."

"They won't, sir."

"Are you sure?"

"Oh, yeah, you don't have to worry about me. I've taken two or three karate classes. I can handle myself quite well, which definitely creates an air of respect."

"Two karate classes?" Mr. Edwards questioned, wanting to laugh and thinking to himself that surely Gunner was joking. He soon realized that Gunner was serious when he saw him standing beside the wall doing a goofy karate chop against the brick! He could hardly keep from laughing any longer.

"Yeah! That's quite impressive!"

"Watch this," Gunner said. He grabbed Mr. Edwards by the wrist with the attitude that he was a real move master.

Mr. Edwards just waited for something to happen, trying desperately not to burst out laughing.

Gunner was really getting into it, while Mr. Edwards wasn't moving or even flinching.

"Feel that?" Gunner exclaimed.

Mr. Edwards shook his head, not feeling a thing.

Gunner, truly believing that all his moves worked, went on to the next one.

"How about this move?"

"No," Mr. Edwards shook his head. This move didn't affect him either. Not wanting to hurt Gunner's feelings, he left him with these last words of advice: "Just be careful with those dangerous karate moves."

Taking all of this seriously, Gunner replied, "Don't you worry. You're looking at a man who would never disrespect the martial arts in any way, shape or form."

"That's comforting," Mr. Edwards said, smiling slightly and still trying not to laugh.

Gunner then turned to address the students, and Mr. Edwards casually removed the sign from Gunner's back and left him there to take care of the class.

Gunner took the volleyball and began to explain different drills to the class. The only reason the kids were listening and trying to take him seriously was because he was an adult. They really would rather be laughing, but his goofiness kept them captivated.

Before Gunner began the exercise, he wanted the kids to loosen up their muscles a bit first. He chose six students, both boys and girls, to come to the front and demonstrate. As they stood shoulder-to-shoulder, he showed them how to do some warm-up exercises. The only difficult thing about the exercise was trying not to laugh at his nasally voice.

A Fighting Chance

"This exercise is very simple, and it's an extraordinarily good movement for loosening up the lower area of the back. Let me show you how this is done. Stand with me, please, if you would."

Gunner joined the line and passed the volleyball to the first kid, who was instructed to pass it to the second, and so on.

"The object of this exercise is to pass it as fast as you can without dropping it, while the twisting motion loosens up your waist area along with various other parts of the upper body." This all seemed very simple, but not when Gunner was involved.

The kids were afraid of dropping the ball, so they passed it very slowly, trying to concentrate. Gunner felt the need to talk and instruct his six volunteers through the entire exercise. By doing this, he remained part of the drill.

"You're doing just great! However, you are never going to get loosened up if you pass it that slowly. Let's pick up the speed and the rest of you, keep your eyes on how this is being done. Especially keep your eyes on me and watch the master at work! This might encourage you to try harder."

The six kids begin to move faster and faster, and those watching were getting a big kick out of it. Gunner's glasses were sliding off his head, but that didn't stop him from putting everything he had into the exercise, looking completely like a total dork! As he became more confident with the kids and himself, Gunner felt comfortable increasing the speed.

"Now, let's move the ball even faster."

The ball finally got back to Gunner. He was so excited that when he twisted to his left, the ball flew out of his hand and got stuck in the scoreboard grate. By then, all the kids were laughing at Gunner. Gunner readjusted his glasses and looked at the stuck ball.

"Well, I guess I just got carried away, that's all. Don't you worry, My Little Friends, it's Mr. Gunner to the rescue!"

Gunner went to get a ladder that was propped up against the wall in a corner of the gym and put it under the scoreboard. He then climbed up the ladder clumsily, instructing as he went along.

"Please take your seats, Kids. Take a deep breath,

and let the oxygen filter through your most exhausted muscles."

Confused, the kids started to take deep breaths and exhale as he instructed.

"That's it, keep breathing," Gunner continued.

The kids concentrated on their breathing while Gunner approached the top step of the ladder. But he realized he still wasn't tall enough to reach the ball. His body was at a full stretch and he was still instructing the kids, "Keep breathing, you're doing very well."

Some of the kids began to shake their heads because they were getting dizzy from breathing in and out so many times.

"Just a couple more," Gunner added. At that moment the ladder slipped out from under him, and he grabbed onto the grate. He was dangling in mid-air. The kids started laughing uncontrollably.

    "Okay...umm. Don't worry," Gunner said while hanging by one hand. "I've got everything under control. Everything is going to be just fine. If someone could just...no, that won't work...well, if we could just...no, that won't work either..." He continued talking to himself, making the kids laugh even harder.

A Fighting Chance

Gunner reached with his left hand to grab the grate. The grate came loose from the wall, leaving Gunner more helpless than before. The kids were rolling on the floor and cracking up. As Gunner reached for the scoreboard, he let go of the grate and hung all of his weight from the board, causing it to come loose from the wall. He was still babbling through all of this while suspended ten feet above the ground. The scoreboard broke away from the wall and hung from the electrical cord, which ran along the entire ceiling and down to an electrical outlet. He reached for the wire, causing it to break loose from the ceiling, one clip at a time, bringing him closer and closer to the ground. The kids laughed even harder as he swung like Tarzan awkwardly but safely to the ground.

Once he hit the ground, the ball fell out of the grate, which was still dangling from the wall, right into Gunner's hands. Gunner didn't miss a beat.

"Now, where were we?" Gunner said, as he resumed teaching. The kids began to cheer and clap for Gunner, who had just made what seemed to be a simple task a very complicated one, not to mention that the ceiling and wall were totally messed up.

Chapter 6

Something's Going Wrong

At the far end of the building, three police officers and two of the school's security police made their way into the gym where all the kids and Gunner were assembled. Mr. Edwards came in from his office as well. Gunner immediately addressed Mr. Edwards.

"I'd like to apologize, Mr. Edwards. The scoreboard incident was an accident. I will be willing to help repair it; however, I don't feel it was necessary to bring the police in on it."

"Relax, Gunner," Mr. Edwards replied seriously. "They're not here for you."

Two of the officers approached Mr. Gunner and Mr. Edwards. The remaining officers covered the exits. The kids, along with Gunner, were curious to know what was going on. Officer Miller addressed the two teachers.

A Fighting Chance

"Pardon the interruption," he said politely to the two teachers as he turned to address the kids. "Mr. Benjamin Wilson, please step forward."

Ben, the kid who had still been in the locker room earlier when Mr. Gunner came in, stood up, red-faced and flushed with fear. He looked around, thought about running, but saw that all the exits were blocked. The officers grabbed his arms and led him to an open area. Officer Miller began to read him his rights while another officer cuffed him.

Ben began to shake and cry at the same time, questioning the officers.

"What are you going to do with me? Am I going to jail? Are you going to tell my parents?"

"All of the above, " Officer Miller sternly answered and then led Ben out of the gym.

Mr. Edwards watched as they left, then turned toward Gunner. "That kid has never been in trouble before. I don't know what possessed him to bring marijuana to school, but he's going to pay now. I'm sure he's headed to juvenile hall."

"Couldn't someone have spent some time with him and counseled him?" Gunner asked innocently.

"Maybe, but that's not how it works anymore these days."

Gunner Is Called to the Office

Gunner was sitting in the principal's office biting his nails, knowing he was in deep trouble for something. His legs began to shake as the principal talked to him.

"About your little accident in the gym. We have a facilities department who could have taken care of this matter in a safer and less costly manner, Mr. Gunner. It's a good thing that neither you nor any of the children got hurt. The problem is that we don't have it in our budget to get the scoreboard fixed. Mr. Gunner, these mistakes are not acceptable in our school. Is that clear?"

"Yes, Miss Ward," he answered in his high-pitched voice again. "And, I can assure you that—"

He was abruptly cut off.

"Whatever, Mr. Gunner! Just don't let it happen again!"

Gunner acted so nervous that he was sweating. He pointed to the paper towel dispenser at the juice service area near her desk and asked permission to take one. "May I?"

Miss Ward was so disgusted that she didn't even say anything. She just nodded and began to shuffle papers on her desk.

Gunner tried to pull one towel off the roll and the whole roll came undone. Miss Ward placed her head in her hands and was ready to explode.

"Don't you worry, Miss Ward. Let me just roll it back—"

"Please, Mr. Gunner!" she said, trying to keep her patience. "Just leave!"

"This will only take a minute," Gunner insisted. As he began to roll up the towels, the entire roll fell off the dispenser and broke a bunch of glasses on the juice service bar. He was startled by this and accidentally hit a section of books, knocking them off the shelf. He innocently looked at Miss Ward, who was staring at him with no expression on her face. He knew that he had made a big mess of things in her office and realized that he should probably leave before he ended up destroying everything.

"I'm leaving now, Miss Ward. Have a marvelous day." He shut the door behind him and a picture fell off the wall and crashed to the floor.

Chapter 7

Study Hall

The bell rang and eight kids came into the classroom and took their seats. It wasn't a very large class. As a matter of fact, these eight kids had no idea that, after today, their lives would never be the same. Adam, Kelly, Billy, DJ, Josh, Dominique, Jackie and Yuri all had their attention on the blackboard where Gunner was writing his name for them…and what looked like his entire family history, too!

Most of the kids in this class didn't know each other very well, so they were all sitting quietly, waiting for the class to start. The second bell rang and Gunner immediately put the chalk down, grabbed the pointer and began to address the class.

"It's a great pleasure to have all of you in my study hall class. I would like to meet all of you and get to know you, but first I would like to tell you a little bit about myself."

DJ leaned over to Billy and whispered, "You've got to be kidding! He expects us to sit and listen to him while he gives us his family history?"

"No way, Man!" Billy answered.

Jackie overheard the conversation between Billy and DJ and leaned back in her chair. She nodded to Billy for him to get Adam's attention.

Billy, knowing what Jackie had in mind right off the bat, quietly got Adam's attention. Adam acknowledged Billy and smiled, realizing what Billy was trying to convey.

Mr. Gunner had no idea what was going on. He began his never-ending story, pointing to each item as he spoke.

"As you all know, my name is Mr. Gunner. I live in the metro area and I am single."

"Gee, that's quite a shock," Yuri quietly said, giggling as always.

"I have no children, and I share expenses with a roommate. His name is Aldo and he is my cousin on my mother's side. Now, to get deeper into my family background, I have no brothers or sisters. I am an only child."

"Thank God there isn't any more of him!" Jackie commented to herself.

The students were getting fidgety as Gunner continued.

"As you can see, on this side of the board, I have fourteen aunts and uncles on my mother's side. No...that's not correct. Hold on, let me think about this for a minute."

The eight kids just couldn't take any more of this. Billy nodded to Adam. While Gunner was talking to himself, Adam activated the laser scan for the whole board. All eight of the kids knew what was about to happen, so when Adam hit the switch, no one would act any differently. Adam signaled that the laser was ready and Billy gave the nod to hit the switch.

The kids waited anxiously for what would happen next. Adam thumbed the little red button and, within an instant, all the chalk writing fell off the board down to the catch tray. There was not a single word or letter left on the board.

The plan worked and Mr. Gunner was still talking to himself. The kids played it calmly and innocently, in great anticipation of the reaction from Mr. Gunner when he saw the board with no writing on it anymore.

"No, I remember that the fourteen aunts and uncles are not on my mother's side but on my father's side as you can see—" Gunner turned to point to the board and was left dumbfounded at the sight of a blank board.

He stared at the board, then at the kids, and back and forth for a time. As much as he usually talked, it would seem as if he'd have a million questions. But this time, the cat got his tongue! He glanced one last time at the board and then continued as if everything were normal. He asked Jackie her name.

Jackie didn't flinch, crack a smile, or anything. She just answered the question.

"I'm Jackie. I like sports, and I am always aware of what is going on around me. I am here to make up work, since I was out for a while from breaking my leg playing rugby."

"Well, that's great." Gunner pointed to the next kid, "And you?"

"Billy. Not Bill. Just Billy. I like working with computers. I'm doing input for the school office. I bring a computer with me everywhere I go, like the one here on my desk."

"Wonderful," Gunner added, showing real interest.

Kelly didn't wait for an invitation to speak. She took the liberty of introducing herself. "Kelly, not Kel...just Kelly," with a cutesy smile, as she mocked Billy. Billy just shook it off as Kelly continued to happily express more information about herself.

"I'm a cheerleader...well...not yet. I will be one next year."

"Well, that's cheerful," Gunner added. "How about you, Young Lady?" he pointed to Dominique.

"I'm Dominique."

"That's a beautiful name. Do you have any hobbies or talents?"

"I like to sing and dance."

Adam was thinking that if Dominique started singing, she might never stop. "Please don't get her started, Mr. Gunner…by the way, I am Adam. There is not a teacher in this country who has a greater IQ than me. I'm far beyond any college professor, but my parents won't let me skip a grade because they want me to be a normal kid. I usually use this class to come up with new inventions. I have six of them patented already."

"He really isn't normal, that's for sure," Jackie casually informed Mr. Gunner.

Josh, sitting behind Adam, realized that Mr. Gunner was just going down the row calling kids in order, and that he was next. Josh was very shy and usually didn't speak unless it was necessary. So he decided to volunteer a bit of information about himself before Gunner called on him.

"I'm Josh. I have a lot of interests, but mainly the environment and its safety. I don't really talk much."

"Unless you forget to recycle," DJ rudely interrupted, chuckling.

"I like to be called DJ. That's short for Dwayne Junior. I don't like Dwayne, so please call me DJ. I like to play just about every sport, which I'd like to be doing in this school right now, but my parents won't let me participate in another sport until I finish a report on a project they have me doing. Every sibling in our family has to turn in a full report to my father on our African-American heritage before we enter high school. I'm taking this class to finish the project so I can play basketball next season. Basically, I'm just a fun-loving, charming guy."

The rest of the class just about gagged on that statement! DJ had a great sense of humor, and he was the kind of kid who didn't care if you made fun of him. In fact, sometimes, he would set you up so that the joke would come back on him. Everybody liked DJ.

Yuri was next, and he just laughed. It wasn't really a laugh; it was more like a quiet, shy giggle. Gunner was looking at him and the rest of the class waited for Yuri to say something. He just kept laughing and it got the rest of the kids to start laughing, too. Gunner didn't get it and he looked around the room with a confused, goofy stare.

"I don't get it. What's so funny?"

Kelly spoke up to answer Gunner's question. She felt the need to pull the class back to order, not to mention, another chance to be in the spotlight. Kelly just loved people and that's why she always needed to get attention.

"Nothing's funny, Mr. Gunner. Yuri laughs at everything. He's an artist. If he can see it, he can draw it."

The other kids spoke out, confirming what Kelly was saying about Yuri's artistic abilities.

Gunner got the class back under control by clapping his hands together in his ever-so-nerdy way.

"Well, this is great. It's good to see all of you enjoying yourselves. Okay, I understand that everyone is here in study hall for different reasons. However, since today is my first day with you, please feel free to gather into groups and just talk quietly amongst yourselves."

The kids shook their heads, thinking that this guy was at least half cool for allowing them to talk in study hall. They got up and moved around the room, visiting with each other while Gunner studied the chalkboard, trying to figure out how the stuff he had written up there got erased.

Outside the classroom, Mrs. Rossenheimer peered through the window to evaluate Mr. Gunner's progress. She had a serious, stern look on her face. Her eyes were like laser beams piercing the room. After a moment, she slipped away, unnoticed.

"Billy, DJ, Kelly and Jackie all sat together. Adam, who normally kept to himself, got up his nerve and headed over to join the foursome.

"Hey, do you guys mind if I join you?"

Jackie saw the opportunity to tease Adam a little.

"Don't you have an underwater car to invent or something? I'm just kidding, park it!" Adam did so with a smile of acceptance.

"There is something weird about Mr. Gunner," Billy expressed with concern.

"That's hard to believe," Jackie answered sarcastically.

"No, I mean really weird. Like every night at about five he goes to a gym. What would he be doing at a gym?" Billy questioned on a serious note.

Kelly felt a need to comment, "All right, what gym

does he go to, and how do you know about this, Billy?"

Billy pulled his chair closer to the group and brought his voice down to just a whisper. "I was doing my input this morning in the office and there was an emergency number listed on his records. Out of curiosity I called it and it was a gym. They said he's there every day around five p.m."

DJ didn't understand the big concern, "What's the big deal about a guy going to a gym? Most people do nowadays. Maybe the guy wants to improve... well...you know..." He pointed to Gunner, who was trying desperately to move his desk from one spot to another. He was struggling so hard, and it wasn't budging, even though it was on rollers.

Billy didn't agree with DJ's comment and Jackie didn't really care. Adam decided to offer his idea in hopes that someone would be interested.

"Do you guys want to find out for sure what's going on?"

They all stopped and gave their undivided attention to Adam, curious to see what was on the mind of the genius.

"How do you propose to do that?" Billy asked.

Adam pulled this little plastic device out of his shirt pocket, about the size of a pea. It was pliable and soft, but paper-thin. They all got close to inspect this thing. It was so tiny that it was almost invisible.

"This is a micro-plastic, long-range radio

transmitter and location device. Are any of you doing anything after school today?"

They all took a moment to think about this, then gave him a unanimous "No!"

"Okay. There is a gym four blocks from the school on Maitland Street. If this is the right gym, why don't you guys meet me there on your bikes?"

Most of the group realized that it was a little too far for them to ride their bikes except Billy.

"I can. It's only two blocks from my house. But how will we know that this is the gym for sure?"

"That's where this little transmitter device comes in. You see that watch Gunner is wearing?" They all took a quick look.

Adam began to explain the plan. "I'm going to stick this device on the face of his watch, so wherever he goes, I can track him. At five o'clock today, if he is at the gym, it will show up on my tracking map."

"You're a genius," Billy said.

"It took you this long to figure that out? I'll call you after school, Billy."

At this point, Mr. Gunner closed the shades on the window near his desk since the glare from the sun was making it uncomfortable for him to read. But before he shut them completely, he glanced out the window and saw a car driving by very slowly in front of the school. There was something odd about this car that came to a stop for a moment, then continued driving slowly around the school with some gangster-looking kids in it.

Gunner had his attention so completely on this car, that when the school bell rang, the kids said good-bye to him and raced out the door. He didn't acknowledge them at all. His mind was completely on the car as it pulled into the parking lot.

He saw a group of kids heading toward this car. They seemed to make some kind of exchange, then walked off as the car sped away. Gunner shook his head and turned to walk back to his desk. When he looked up, he was shocked to see no one there.

Chapter 8

The Hunt

Adam was nervous and anxiously waiting in front of his house for Billy to show up. He kept looking at his watch and then down the street to see if there was any sign of him. Finally he saw Billy coming around the corner on his bike and motioned for him to hurry.

Slightly out of breath, Billy pulled up and asked Adam what the hurry was all about. "It's not even 4:30 yet. Hey, you know, I didn't even realize I live so close to a brainiac."

Adam didn't answer Billy. He was more interested in the mission they were about to embark upon.

"My tracking device on Gunner shows me that he has been roaming around the gym area for about twenty minutes. I want to get there as soon as possible so we can catch everything on tape."

A Fighting Chance

Billy wrinkled his forehead in confusion. "Tape? Where's the camera?"

Adam pointed to the baseball cap he was wearing, "Right in here."

Billy took a closer look, but still couldn't see anything. "No way, I don't see a camera."

"Believe me, it's there. Let me show you. Watch this."

Adam showed Billy his wristwatch. It turned out to be a video monitor that played back with Billy looking into it, searching for the camera lens. Billy couldn't believe what he was seeing.

"Show me that again."

Adam hit a button on his watch which rewound the tape and replayed Billy's request. Billy was amazed.

"This stuff is incredible, Adam. I think I'm starting to like you."

"Don't get too serious. I've got my eye on Kelly," Adam said jokingly.

Billy laughed and slapped the bill on Adam's hat.

"Hey, watch it! Remember the camera!" Adam said, trying to dodge Billy's gesture.

"Oh yeah, sorry. Hey, I'll race you over there," Billy said, as he took off on his bike, leaving Adam in his dust.

Adam raced off after Billy, but he was not able to go as fast since he was carrying so much equipment in his backpack that it weighed him down.

Billy was about ten or twelve bike lengths ahead of

Adam and kept looking back to see if he was getting any closer. He turned back around and smiled, knowing that Adam would probably never catch up to him.

A smile from ear to ear showed the enjoyment Billy was getting from the wind blowing on his face while racing his bike when, all of a sudden, Adam came whizzing by him. He was not even pedaling! Billy wondered how he did that. Adam noted Billy's confused look and said with a smile, "I have a solar-powered engine on my bike."

Billy continued pedaling until he reached the gym parking lot where Adam was already waiting with his gear all set up.

"What took you so long, Billy?"

"Wise guy!"

Adam began to watch his monitor, which was set up in the middle of his equipment. "Get ready," he said with anticipation. "He's half a block away." They both peered in the same direction, waiting for Mr. Gunner to come into view.

Adam locked in on a Harley Davidson Fatboy motorcycle. The person on the bike was wearing a helmet, leather jacket, jeans and black riding boots. Billy noticed Adam staring at the bike and felt that he was on to something.

"What's the matter, Adam?"

"Somebody must have stolen Mr. Gunner's watch!"

"How do you figure that?"

A Fighting Chance

Adam didn't take his eyes off the bike. He just answered, totally dumbfounded, "Because the transmitter I placed on Mr. Gunner's watch is now being worn by the person riding that Harley Davidson."

"What are we going to do now?"

"We're going to wait for the evidence to unfold."

That wasn't the answer Billy was hoping for.

The Harley pulled into the parking spot and the person dismounted the bike with his back to the boys. As he walked toward the gym, he removed his helmet. The mysterious man entered the gym, and the door closed behind him. Billy started heading toward the door but was quickly stopped by Adam, who had different plans.

"No! Come this way. Follow me!"

They both took off running toward the Harley. Sneaking up to it and stooping down so they wouldn't be seen, Adam quickly opened the saddlebags, looking for something—anything that could be a clue.

"What are you doing?"

"It's cool. I just need to find out who this guy is."

"Hurry!" Billy said nervously, afraid of getting caught.

"Relax. Just keep your eyes open and make sure no one—wait a minute... Bingo! I found it!"

Adam opened some sort of wallet that displayed identification. "Detective Joseph G. something... It's scratched out. I'm sure it's Gunner. He's with the

Narcotics and Homicide Division. He's a cop!"

"No kidding? A *big* time cop, too."

"Come on, let's check him out!" Adam led Billy toward the gym.

"How are we going to know who he is?"

"Don't worry. I've got it covered."

When they got inside the gym, they noticed that there was a very small section designated for lifting weights. Most of the place was for boxing, contrary to what they originally thought.

As they continued looking around, one of the gym workers approached them. "Can I help you?" he asked kindly.

Billy tried to answer, "Uh…"

Realizing that Billy was stuck in confusion, Adam answered the question. "Do you mind if we just watch for a moment?"

"Not at all. Just don't go into the workout areas."

"Yes sir. No problem," Adam answered respectfully.

They both wandered around the gym, keeping an eye on all the various activities going on. In one corner, a man was hitting the heavy bag with such power that the person holding it was having a hard time hanging on. Adam kept his eye on him while he reached into his pocket and pulled out a pair of glasses. He put them on and just shook his head. He was so stunned at what he saw that he just began talking to himself. "Oh, my gosh. I don't believe it."

A Fighting Chance

"Believe what? What are you looking at, Adam?" Billy peered over at the man punching the heavy bag at the same time Adam answered.

"That's him!"

"How do you know?" Billy responded a little unsurely.

Adam removed the glasses from his face and handed them to Billy.

"Here, put these glasses on and look at his neck."

Billy, very curious as to what Adam was talking about, took the glasses and put them on. He looked at the man hitting the punching bag.

"He has pink stuff on his neck," Billy said, not understanding what that meant.

"I marked his neck so I could pick him out in a crowd if I needed to. Mr. Gunner is one bad José," Adam said with respect.

"Whoa. You can say that again."

The two boys just looked at each other, not knowing what to think.

"Don't tell a soul. If he is undercover, we don't want to blow it for him. Tomorrow during study hall we'll pop the question."

"Deal," Billy replied, agreeing with everything Adam said.

Chapter 9

The Uncovering

The next day at Metro Middle School, Billy and Adam made their way behind a tree just left of the front doors of the school. Adam might have been a genius, but he was still a kid. He had the brains of Einstein, but the same childish excitement as his schoolmate, Billy, who stood next to him with incredible anticipation.

The study hall group exited the bus and Adam and Billy motioned for the group to join them for a minute. All of the kids, except for Dominique and Yuri, gathered with them to see what was going on.

"What's up?" DJ asked curiously.

"Hang tight till the rest get here," Adam strongly suggested.

It was so hard for Adam and Billy to hold back all

of their new-found information, that the boys were about to burst.

Jackie waited for Dominique's and Yuri's bus to drop them off. The bus passed right in front of her, but she couldn't help watching the strange-looking car with two guys inside it. Jackie didn't know it, but it was the same car Mr. Gunner had seen the other day. Jackie watched intently, losing track of Dominique's and Yuri's whereabouts altogether. Instead, she focused on a couple of kids walking toward a bush near where the strange car was parked. One kid dropped his schoolbook on the ground, apparently on purpose. He bent over to pick it up, and when he stood back up, he looked over at the guys in the car and nodded to them. Then the two kids walked away. Jackie thought she saw the kid leave something on the ground when he bent over to pick up his book, but she couldn't make it out from where she was standing.

While watching this scenario unfold, Jackie also saw one of the guys in the car get out and go over to the bush to pick up what the kid left on the ground. By then, she began to share what was going on with one of her friends, when Adam interrupted her.

"Here come Dominique and Yuri."

Adam and Billy yelled for them to hurry up. Dominique and Yuri saw the group gathered around the tree and headed quickly over there, knowing that it must be something important for all of them to be together.

They both ran over and arrived out of breath. Dominique fixed her windblown hair and Yuri just smiled as they both waited to hear what was happening.

Billy and Adam both started talking really fast and all at once, telling the gang everything they knew about Gunner.

"I'm telling you, we saw him with our own eyes."

Adam chimed in excitedly, "He's big and strong, and he's got these big arms and was punching the bag so hard that the guy holding it couldn't even hold on."

"What in the world are you talking about?" Jackie asked in a very confused voice.

The whole group felt as completely confused as Jackie. They all had the strangest look on their faces.

Billy exploded with the punch line: "Mr. Gunner is a cop. A detective to be exact!"

They were all speechless; not a word was spoken. Even Yuri was speechless, without a smile on his face. Both Adam and Billy nodded their heads and grinned from ear-to-ear. They both felt that they had uncovered something big.

After a moment, the silence was broken. "So what are we supposed to do now?" Jackie curiously asked.

"Go to Miss Ward and tell her," Dominique said confidently.

"Don't you think she already knows?" said Kelly.

The group didn't even realize that Josh was there until he answered Kelly's question. "No! Miss Ward doesn't know."

A Fighting Chance

"How do you know?" Kelly answered, wondering how she could be so wrong.

Josh talked so softly that the group leaned forward in order to hear every word he said.

"I was in the office when Mr. Gunner first came. They only knew that the school board was sending over another teacher to handle the student increase."

"Here's what we need to do," Adam said, taking charge of the situation. They all gathered around to hear what Adam had to say.

In the Study Hall After the Stake-Out

Jackie was the first one to get to the study hall class.

"Not this stuff again," Jackie said, seeing Mr. Gunner once again writing his family history on the chalkboard. The rest of the kids filed in and took their seats. Gunner was again dressed in sweatpants, dress shoes, a dress shirt and his bow tie.

All eight of the kids could feel the tension rising. They kept looking back and forth at each other nervously, not saying a word.

None of them knew *if* and *when* someone was going to say something to Gunner. They didn't have it planned out. They were just going to let things happen as they happened.

Mr. Gunner, the odd person that he was, stood at the chalkboard with the pointer in his hand, ready to begin his class when the bell rang. The kids weren't saying a word and Gunner just stood, frozen in place. Yuri laughed quietly, since the way Mr. Gunner was standing there was quite funny.

None of the other kids were smiling. They were more concerned about what they were going to say and how they were going to handle it.

The bell rang and Mr. Gunner "unfroze" himself. He began to welcome the class without even looking at them. He was afraid to take his eyes off the chalkboard, considering what happened last time. If the mysterious phenomenon was going to happen like it did the day before, he didn't want to miss it.

"Good morning, Class. It's good to see you all today. Before you get started on your homework, I thought that you might be interested in what I started to show you on the board yesterday, before it...went away! Anyway—"

"Excuse me, Mr. Gunner. What are your thoughts about physical fitness training?" Jackie asked, interrupting Gunner in the middle of his boring speech.

"I think it's good," Gunner answered. "As a matter of fact, it's healthy for the body."

The kids felt that they had broken the ice. Now they felt more confident in asking further questions.

"Do you work out?" Adam threw out to him.

"Occasionally I do," Gunner answered calmly as if nothing was wrong.

Billy felt certain that Gunner would have nothing but a positive response to his next question, so he stood to his feet and asked Gunner, "Can you arm wrestle me, Mr. Gunner? I've been working out for a couple of weeks now and I would like to test my strength."

"Well, I don't see why not," Gunner said. "However, I do have to warn you that my arm is very strong."

Just looking at Gunner's physique made them want to laugh at the comment about his arm, knowing he was not who he said he was.

"You could say that again," Billy whispered to Adam.

Billy smiled at the group and firmly planted himself in the chair that was right next to Gunner's desk. He slammed his arm onto the desk in the ready position. Billy made his stand, and he awaited Gunner's acceptance.

Mr. Gunner pushed up his glasses that repeatedly slipped down his nose and sat down in the proper position to grab Billy's hand.

Billy was really nervous, since he believed this man could probably snap his arm in two. Billy's smile left his face and fear took its place. *What am I doing?* he thought to himself. He started to loosen his grip as if to back out of the deal, when Adam grabbed both of their hands.

"Ready?" Adam asked. "Go!"

The struggle was on and a burst of confidence came over Billy because he realized he was still in the race. His hand had not been slammed through the bottom of the table.

All the kids were cheering Billy on, but neither opponent seemed to be winning.

Poor Mr. Gunner was struggling so hard. His face was turning red and his glasses slowly slid down his nose, while his entire body shook from the intense battle.

Billy was giving it everything he had, but his strength was wearing out. His arm was falling in the losing direction.

Everyone continued to cheer for Billy. Yuri started to laugh because Gunner was cheering for himself.

A Fighting Chance

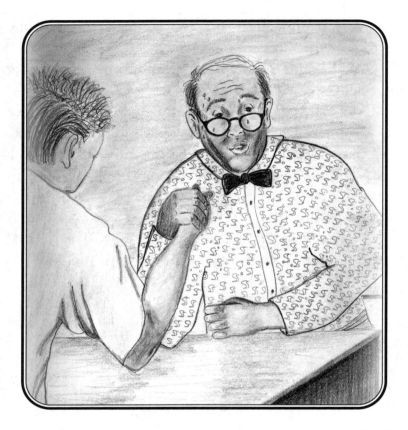

His cheering must have worked, because he finally pinned Billy to the desk.

"Wow! You have quite an amount of arm strength," Gunner said, trying to soften the blow of getting beaten and making sure Billy's feelings weren't hurt.

"Did you give me everything you had?" Billy asked questioningly.

"Of course I did, Billy. Now, Class, let's get back to what I have written on the board."

Adam took a bold stand. "We don't know if we want to hear what you have to say about what you put on the board. What I mean by that is, we don't really feel that it's the truth."

"Oh, I get it. You don't believe I have all of those family members, do you?"

"With all due respect, Sir, we don't believe you are who you say you are," Billy said politely.

Gunner looked puzzled. "Then who am I?" he asked.

"You tell us," Josh said, coming from nowhere.

Everyone turned to look at Josh. They were stunned that he even said anything, especially at a time like this.

Josh gave them a little smile, then focused on waiting for Mr. Gunner to answer him. They were all anxious for his response.

"I don't understand," Gunner said, confused.

Nobody knew what to say, so Billy passed it off to Adam, who always seemed to have the right answer.

"Adam might be able to explain it better for you, Sir."

"Well, you see, it's like this," Adam continued.

"Billy was working on the computer yesterday, and—"

Billy interrupted Adam, feeling confident now that he could take it from there. "And I found an unusual phone number that belongs to a gym, and—"

Then DJ cut in, "We were kind of wondering what you did there."

Billy continued, "So I called the gym. I know I'm not supposed to do that, Sir, but it *is* a gym!"

Gunner smiled, "Well, of course it is. I like to work out and do my calisthenics there."

Adam, not believing a word Gunner was saying, continued. "Well, that's not all we did. Here, look." Adam peeled the tracking device off of his watch and then showed Gunner what it represented. "This is an invention of mine. It's a tracking device. It pinpoints your location exactly, and we waited for you at the gym."

Billy chimed in, "I went with him. We watched you ride in on a Harley Davidson. Then we went inside and watched you train."

Gunner started to laugh when he realized that they had interpreted everything completely wrong.

"You guys are something else! What you saw was my roommate. He must have borrowed my watch and must have gone to the gym. Silly kids! I definitely have to give you credit for trying."

The other kids started chastising Billy and Adam for getting them all excited for nothing. Jackie just shook her head in disgust at Billy for having such a ridiculous thought. All the kids thought that they had been had and began to yell simultaneously at Billy and Adam. The boys couldn't understand anything they were saying because of the many remarks that were being thrown at them, one right after the other.

"I believe Billy and Adam," said Josh, silencing the crowd.

"What did you say?" DJ responded to him in shock.

Josh repeated what he said. "I believe Billy and Adam."

"Why?" Jackie asked.

"Thank you, Josh, I will explain," Adam said, defending himself.

"Here, Mr. Gunner, please put these glasses on."

Mr. Gunner had no idea what these kids were doing, but he felt that he should just play along. Without resistance, he gladly put on the glasses.

"These are nice glasses, but they are kind of dark. What are they for?"

Adam just handed Gunner a mirror. "Look at your neck in this mirror," Adam said, assuming a scientist-like identity.

"Would you look at that!" Gunner remarked. "It looks like I've got some paint on my neck."

Adam then presented his evidence. "That's not paint, Mr. Gunner. I marked your neck with invisible ink that can only be seen with these glasses. I saw it in the movie *Mission Impossible*. When we went in the gym, I put on the glasses and looked around the room.

There was a man beating the stuffing out of a punching bag and he had the same mark on his neck as you do, Detective Gunner. I also videotaped all of this."

Silence fell over the room. The six other kids who were picking on Billy and Adam were so still from disbelief that you could almost hear their hearts beating as they waited with mouths agape for some sort of response from Mr. Gunner.

Gunner put his head down for a moment to gather his thoughts. He had been uncovered by a small group of middle school students.

How could this be happening? he thought to himself. A thousand thoughts flew through his head, but he knew he had to give them some sort of answer. He realized that the truth was the only way out.

These eight kids were about to hear Gunner speak in a masculine voice—one that would not fit the look that he displayed.

What will their reaction be? Gunner contemplated no longer.

"So!" he said with a masculine voice.

At this point, all the kids just stared at him in complete shock. They were all speechless. Dominique put her hand over her mouth, trying not to scream.

"Well, you figured out who I am. That's quite impressive work, Billy and Adam," Gunner said, using his own deep voice.

Kelly asked a serious question in a very shaky voice.

"So what are you going to do to us now that we

know who you are?"

Gunner rested his chin on his folded hands. In spite of his dorky outfit, his eyes remained serious. He was not the same man they were talking to just a few minutes ago.

"I'm going to have to kill each of you, one at a time."

Gunner didn't flinch at the comment he just made, but the kids gasped for air, feeling as though it might be their last breath. They didn't know what to do or think, whether to run or stand there and scream. After a moment, Gunner cracked a smile and the kids began to breathe again.

Dominique still had her hand over her mouth. She wouldn't take it away.

"I know one thing," Gunner continued. "If none of you say anything I can keep on doing what I came here to do."

Adam and Billy were quick to respond, only Adam got it out first.

"We didn't say anything. Promise!"

"Are you surprised, Dominique?" Gunner replied.

She didn't take her hand off her mouth. She just nodded.

"Why would she be surprised?" Adam asked, wrinkling his forehead.

"Tell them," Gunner said, with his hands folded calmly in front of him.

Dominique pulled her hand away from her mouth

and in a very high voice she squeaked out, "He's my dad."

"Your what!" they all said at the same time.

"He's my dad and his last name is Galardi, not Gunner."

That's why the rest of the name was scratched out on the photo ID, Adam thought to himself.

"It must remain Gunner as long as I am here. Dominique, you didn't think your dad would be working on a case at your school, did you?"

Dominique, still quite stunned, just nodded.

The group decided that it was time to get more information and left it up to Adam to question Gunner, since Adam was always one step ahead of everyone else. Adam felt that one chapter of this mystery had been solved and he was ready to solve the next one. He proceeded without fear, loving the challenge.

"So, what did you come here to do?" Adam asked.

Joseph Gunner—or Galardi—began to open up to the kids. He contemplated for a moment whether he should reveal this information or not. Not sensing any reasons why not, he began to explain.

"Remember yesterday's drug bust? There is a supplier who deals to these kids and my job is to find out who the supplier is. However, I saw something yesterday that bothered me."

"What was it?" Yuri asked with a smile.

Gunner smiled back at him. He studied Yuri for a moment and realized that Yuri's laugh was a reaction of his shyness. When he laughed, it covered up any embarrassment that he felt from things he said.

Gunner continued, "The kid who was arrested, Ben, didn't need handcuffs. He needed someone who could have reached him earlier and led him to different choices. What bothers me is that he is not the only kid who needs this sort of attention. Sometimes, there just isn't a way to help kids in time before disaster strikes. Then, when they get busted, the state gets them, and it's downhill all the way after that."

Adam's mind was running a hundred miles an hour, knowing he was ready for a challenge.

"What if I told you that I could help you get to these kids in time and you could do your stuff?"

Gunner knew that he was talking to a thirteen-year-old. All kids have imaginations that are mainly fantasy. Gunner didn't want to kill Adam's imagination, so he gave him a chance to explain further.

"I'm listening."

Adam knew what he was capable of and what he was about to suggest. He had no doubt that he could back it all up. He reached into his large briefcase to pull out a device. "With this little baby..." he said without even looking. "No, this is the wrong one," Adam realized he had pulled out a different device.

"Show him what that one does," Jackie said with a smile.

All the kids were anxious to see Mr. Gunner's

reaction when he found out how he had been tricked yesterday.

"Watch the chalkboard," Adam said, warming up the device.

Gunner slowly turned to look behind him at the chalkboard. With a smile, Adam hit the little red button. All the writing on the board granulated and fell to the catch tray. The entire board was erased in a split second. Gunner turned back to face Adam, but he didn't say a word. He realized that Adam was not an average kid. He was simply a genius.

"So that's how the board got erased yesterday."

Adam now had Gunner's undivided attention. He reached into the same bag and pulled out a small device similar in size and shape to the one he just demonstrated. "This is what I was looking for," Adam exclaimed. "This contraption can be used to pinpoint anything you want, from smoke to bad breath—you name it. I can program it to locate drugs of any kind. It's like an electronic dog sniffer."

"Are you serious?" Gunner asked, concerned about something like this really working.

"He wouldn't lie to you," Billy said with confidence, having seen Adam in action.

"Hey, wait a minute," Billy added. "I could pull up records on kids regarding their background, even their family history or something."

Adam interrupted Billy, not paying attention to

anything he had said. "Second floor, locker thirty-two, top shelf, a dime bag of marijuana and exactly two-thirds of an ounce of cocaine."

Everyone looked at Adam strangely.

"What are you talking about?" Kelly asked.

Adam wondered what they didn't understand. He then realized that they had been talking about something else while he had been concentrating on his scheme. He then explained to them what he was talking about.

"Sorry. I was in my own little world for a moment there. I programmed this little machine and it already hit the jackpot."

Gunner buried his head in his hands.

"This is unbelievable. Hang on, I could actually use you guys. Wait a minute, what am I talking about? I can't endanger you kids. I wouldn't have to, or would I?"

All the kids looked as confused as Gunner had just sounded.

"Would you like to let us in on your little conversation with yourself, Dad?" Dominique asked.

He replied, "No! Yes! Yes, of course. First, I must have your word that none of you will breathe a word of this to anyone."

They were so excited and, at the same time, couldn't believe what was happening. Of course they all agreed to Mr. Gunner's demand.

"How can I trust you?" Gunner reluctantly asked.

"You're bigger than we are. You'll kill us if we

squeal," Yuri said out of nowhere, causing everyone to laugh.

"You're right," Gunner said with a kidding smile. "I'm not here to hurt anyone, just to give a fighting chance to anyone who needs it."

Without even taking a breath, Gunner went back to talking in the goofy voice of his alter ego. "So just get back to your seats and utilize this time wisely."

At first the kids were startled by Mr. Gunner's immediate transformation, but they soon realized why he changed identities. They had been so engrossed in what they were talking about that they didn't realize Mrs. Rossenheimer had come into their classroom.

Mrs. Rossenheimer addressed Gunner as the kids made their way back to their seats.

"Mr. Gunner, Miss Ward would like to see you in her office immediately. I'll watch your class."

"Oh yes, of course, I'll get over there right away, Mrs. Rossenpotter."

"The name is pronounced *Rossenheimer*, not *Rossenpotter*," she said.

"Oh, yes, I'm sorry," Gunner said as he caught his foot on the side of the desk, causing papers to go flying everywhere.

"Now who put that desk in the middle of the room?"

The kids laughed, knowing that he was just acting. As Gunner opened the door, he turned to the kids and gave them a wink, as if to say that the incident that just happened was for their laughing pleasure.

DJ continued to laugh and leaned over to Dominique.

"How does he make his voice do that?"

Dominique just rolled her eyes at the question. She thought about how her dad acted like this all the time, but it was still funny to her. She was glad that her friends liked him.

Mrs. Rossenheimer began talking to the class when she was interrupted by a very loud crash down the hall. Gunner had run into something and he probably did it on purpose, knowing it would make the kids laugh in front of the stiff-necked Mrs. Rossenheimer.

Joseph Galardi would never do anything to disrespect a teacher, but he enjoyed bringing laughter and a smile to a kid's face.

"Are you enjoying Mr. Gunner's class?" Mrs. Rossenheimer asked after shaking her head at the sound of Gunner's last crash.

The response she got from all the kids was more than positive.

Chapter 10

Keeping Gunner's Identity While Taking the Next Step

Mr. Gunner entered Miss Ward's office in his nerdy character, slamming the door behind him. The slamming of the door caused another picture to fall off the wall. That really seemed to push Miss Ward over the edge.

"Mr. Gunner, carefully have a seat. Try not to break anything, please!"

Always in character, he responded to her remark, "I won't break anything. It's just a cushioned chair. I can't see how it would break, that is unless there is a faulty leg or—"

"Mr. Gunner!" Miss Ward sternly and abruptly cut him off.

A Fighting Chance

"Yes, Miss Ward," he meekly answered.

"Just listen. Don't speak and don't touch anything. Just listen."

"Yes, ma—"

"Now see, that's speaking. Not a word, please!"

She was silent for a moment, took a deep breath and then continued, hoping it gave Gunner time to let what she said sink in.

"Mr. Gunner, you have been here for only two days and I have had more complaints from teachers about you than I have had with any of my staff the entire time I have been here. My nephew, Ryles McKenzie, said that, earlier today, you almost broke his arm when you opened your classroom door. These kids should not have to come to school not knowing if they are going to return home in one piece. Just so you know, I have requested a transfer replacement for you as soon as possible. Fortunately for you, with the student growth in the metro area, there is no one available to replace you, but as soon as there is, I hope we are first on the list. Mr. Gunner, I insist that you take the rest of the day off. That will be all, Mr. Gunner."

Like a puppy with his tail between his legs, Gunner got up from his seat and headed toward the door, knowing he had to act like that so his cover would not be blown. He turned back toward Miss Ward and extended a polite apology.

"You probably won't accept this, but I would like to apologize for any inconvenience I have caused you and the faculty."

Miss Ward, being the sweet and compassionate person that she was, started feeling bad for coming down so hard on poor Mr. Gunner. Although by now, Mr. Gunner had closed the door ever so gently and left her thinking about what she just said to him. She reviewed in her mind that her actions were out of impulse and instant anger rather than from thoughtfulness and discipline. She decided to call Mr. Gunner back into the room and apologize when she heard a scream and clanging just outside her door.

She looked out her office window and saw that Mr. Gunner had fallen onto the school receptionist's desk and her cup of water had spilled all over her lap. Miss Ward just shook her head and went back to her desk thinking that she had done the right thing with Mr. Gunner after all.

Galardi's Meeting With the Police Captain

Captain Williams, the police captain, was rather passive compared to the impression we usually have when we think of police captains—loud and short-tempered. He and Joseph had known each other for a long time and they both had a lot of respect for one another.

"You're not feeding me a line now, are you?" Captain Williams said to Joseph.

"This genius kid, Adam, did all this on his own?"

Joseph answered the question honestly. "Yeah. Well, he had help from seven other kids and some technology that no one else has."

"You might have something there, Galardi. Will these kids be in any sort of danger by helping you?"

"No, sir. I'll make sure of it," Galardi answered, taking full responsibility.

"Galardi, I have no reason to doubt or second-guess you. You are doing a great job as always. You might be onto something good. Keep me posted. Let me know if there is anything I can do to help."

Back in the Classroom

The class was about to end and Mrs. Rossenheimer had told the kids that Mr. Gunner would not be returning until after class. She had also told them that if they were in the middle of something with Mr. Gunner, it would have to wait until tomorrow, when he returned.

"Mrs. Rossenheimer," Adam said after raising his hand.

"Yes, Adam?"

"It's ten minutes before the bell and usually we are allowed to talk quietly. Do you mind if we do that?"

"I guess not. Quietly, please."

"Yes, ma'am," Adam responded, surprised that she agreed.

All the kids figured Adam had a plan and huddled

around him as he, the brainiac, had become the focal point of this operation. Adam handed out little pieces of paper to everyone, explaining what was on his mind.

"Listen up, this is my address, directions and phone number, in case anyone gets lost."

"What are we supposed to do with this?" Jackie asked.

"I'm sorry, guys. I am ahead of myself again. I want all of us to meet tonight at my house after dinner, say about six. Does anyone have a problem with that?"

It seemed that everyone could make it. They all were committed, realizing that this wasn't a kid's fantasy but a real exciting mission.

Of course Jackie had to give Adam a hard time. "I'll be there as long as I can get my homework done first."

"How much homework do you have?" Adam asked.

"None, yet," Jackie said, causing everyone to laugh softly so that Mrs. Rossenheimer didn't get upset.

"Just get it done and be there," Adam told her like a parent would.

Adam had proven himself beyond what any of them would have expected and they were willing to listen to his ideas and whatever he had to say.

At about that time, Mr. Gunner made a surprisingly loud entrance into the classroom.

"Excuse me, Mrs. Rossenheimer."

A Fighting Chance

"What are you doing back here? I thought Miss Ward asked you to take the rest of the day off."

The bell rang and Mrs. Rossenheimer headed toward the door. She couldn't wait to leave Mr. Gunner's presence. She was not normally a very happy person anyway, so if anyone gave her a reason to be miserable, she would take it.

"She did ask me to take the rest of the day off, but I forgot my briefcase. Thanks for taking the class, Mrs. Rossenheimer. I hope the kids didn't give you any trouble."

"The *kids* are not a problem," Mrs. Rossenheimer said with her unpleasant attitude as she stormed out the door.

"Oh yeah, she really likes you, Dad!" Dominique said in a defensive tone.

"Some people are like that. You react by being nice to them, not by using their tone of voice," Gunner said.

"You're right, I'm sorry," Dominique answered respectfully.

"See you guys later," Mr. Galardi said to the kids as they left the classroom.

These eight kids definitely had their creative energy flowing and were excited to be part of something meaningful.

Joseph Galardi began his nerdy Mr. Gunner act again and walked through the hallway where the crowds were beginning to thin out a little. He spotted Ryles McKenzie, Miss Ward's nephew. He figured that he should apologize to the young man, so that it might take some tension off of him and Miss Ward.

Ryles was at his locker when he saw Mr. Gunner heading his way.

"Ryles!" Mr. Gunner yelled out in his goofy voice.

Ryles quickly shut his locker just before Gunner arrived. Gunner sensed that Ryles seemed nervous about something. Maybe he had a hard time in his last class. However, when Gunner reached him, everything seemed to be all right.

"What can I do for you, Mr. Gunner?"

"Nothing, actually. I would like to apologize for nearly breaking your arm the other day. I did have total control of the door and I wanted to tell you that you were not in any danger, although your aunt was quite upset with me. I just wanted to apologize."

"No problem. Everything's cool. Thanks for the apology."

Ryles didn't stick around. He scooted out of there very quickly. Joseph smiled and felt satisfied with the apology that Ryles had accepted. Too bad his aunt isn't as understanding, he thought to himself. As he walked off, he glanced at Ryles's locker and focused on the locker number, which happened to be thirty-two. That was the locker number that Adam pulled up on his little device. He realized that this was the locker that supposedly had all the drugs in it.

Galardi knew that this was not the time to bust open a locker, nor did he want to do that at this point. Something did have to be done, but it would have to wait for the right moment. Just then, all Galardi was worried about was getting out of the building before Miss Ward saw him and asked him what he was still doing there.

Galardi got into his Mr. Gunner character again and headed toward the front door of the school, hoping that

Miss Ward didn't pop up from nowhere. He walked faster and faster after he spotted Mrs. Rossenheimer, who had probably seen him and was going to tell Miss Ward that he was in the building. He made it out the front door and ran to his little "wanna be" car that was given to him strictly for this assignment.

Miss Ward did see him as she peered out of her office window. She closely watched to see that no disaster followed. Once he got into the car and started it up, she grabbed her school walkie-talkie and radioed to the staff members in the parking lot who were directing bus traffic to get out of Gunner's way, just in case.

"To all staff in the parking lot, Mr. Gunner is backing out of his parking space and will be leaving the property. Please make sure he doesn't hit anybody or anything. Thank you."

By doing this, she felt that she had covered all of her bases to make sure there were no more disasters at the school. She made her way back to her desk to finish some paperwork before she called it a day.

Chapter 11

Meeting at Adam's House

A dam, there are plenty more crackers if your friends want them without cheese," his mother said with a servant's heart.

Jackie still had her shin pads on from soccer practice. She was sitting on the floor, about to crash from exhaustion. DJ stared at Jackie for a moment, the wheels in his head spinning. Jackie eventually closed her eyes and took a few Z's before their meeting actually started. DJ couldn't take it anymore. Jackie's mouth was open as if she were about to snore. DJ got up, walked over to her and put his entire finger in her mouth, startling her. She harmlessly gagged and jumped to her feet. Everyone started laughing hysterically. Jackie bopped DJ on the head and, at the same time, the doorbell rang.

They all roared with laughter at how funny it was

when the bop and the bell happened at exactly the same time, as if to suggest that DJ's head was empty and just rang when it was hit!

Dominique and Kelly were singing some sort of song that no one recognized as they entered the house dancing and singing.

"Come on in, Girls," Adam's mother said as she welcomed them. "Find a seat anywhere you can. There's plenty of food. Just help yourselves."

"Thank you. I'm Dominique."

"You're welcome. And you must be Kelly. Adam has told me a lot about you."

Adam was on the other side of the room giving his mother a cross look, suggesting that she not say anymore. She smiled as she realized that she was not supposed to say that to Kelly. She made it worse by saying to Adam, "Oh, I'm sorry, Honey. I didn't realize you didn't want me to say anything to her."

"That's all right, Mrs. Leist," Kelly said, somewhat embarrassed.

"Sometimes I say things when I'm not supposed to. Okay, Kids, I'll just go make myself useful in the kitchen, and you guys enjoy yourselves."

"Thanks, Mom," Adam said, relieved that she was leaving the room.

Jackie gave him a little smack on the shoulder. "Don't disrespect your mother with that tone of voice. She is a sweet lady."

"Okay, okay, I'm sorry."

All these kids who really didn't know each other that well a couple of days ago were now becoming friends and learning about each other. This bonding that none of them were aware of was developing a team like no other in history.

"Why are we all here?" DJ asked.

"I've got an idea that just might work," Adam replied. "Do you remember when Mr. Gunner said that if he could get to the kids before the problem, it would be more beneficial for their futures?"

They all nodded, acknowledging that they remembered and Adam continued.

"If I could show you a way to do this, would you be willing to be part of this?"

They all looked at each other, not really knowing what in the world Adam had up his sleeve or what to say. They all agreed, "Sure, why not?"

They really didn't know what they were agreeing to, but it sounded like a lot of fun and it sure seemed to be stirring up excitement of the unknown.

"Follow me," Adam said as he stood up and headed toward the basement.

The basement was Adam's domain. It was the place where he could let his mind run freely. No one was at his level of intelligence and if he didn't have this place to create, he would go crazy.

All eight of them carefully and curiously made their way down the stairs into the dark basement. At the bottom Adam reached for the light switch, but didn't turn it on. He remembered that he was with eighth graders who didn't understand things as he did. Actually, no one had ever seen what Adam was about to show these seven kids.

"Before I turn this light on and expose what you are about to see, you must first promise me that you will tell absolutely no one. Is that a promise?"

At this point they were so curious that they would agree to anything Adam asked them. They all agreed.

Adam felt comfortable with their response and flipped the switch. The seven kids were quite still—not a word, not a blink, not a move. Adam smiled proudly, knowing that they were impressed. With that in mind, he felt that he would be able to run this project successfully.

Even though the seven kids had never seen a laboratory before, they knew they were looking at the most incredible one ever made.

Tubes, wires, gizmos, lights, buttons and gadgets were all over the room. Billy finally blinked and began breathing again. He couldn't wait to ask Adam what all of this was.

"You are a genius!" Kelly exclaimed in awe.

"Thank you," Adam added with a proud smile.

Adam continued as Josh began walking around, inspecting the lab curiously.

"Now, let me tell you why you are here."

They all listened intently, giving their complete attention to Adam.

"When Mr. Gunner finds out what we can do, he's going to want us to team up with him."

"I know my dad. We're just kids. He's not going to want our help," Dominique added reluctantly.

"We may just be kids," Adam said, "but I can promise you this: there is no adult anywhere, in the government of the United States or any other country, that has what I have down here. I don't mean to boast, but it's the truth."

"Why haven't you told important people about this stuff?" Jackie asked.

"I don't want it to fall into the wrong hands," Adam replied, as he continued.

"Listen, I need each of you to play a part. All of us have a special gift and it's time to use them all together."

A Fighting Chance

Josh glanced at an empty milk jug in the trashcan. He questioned Adam in his shy, polite but stern way.

"Why are you throwing this away? You should recycle it and reuse it again."

Without giving Josh an answer, Adam continued. "See what I mean? If we work together, we can help Mr. Gunner do exactly what he said couldn't be done. Now give me a hand and help me gather the equipment that we are going to need for tomorrow."

Everyone was eager to take part in whatever Adam asked them to do. Adam, just one week ago, was a kid who was laughed at and made fun of for being so smart. He now had not only organized a team of eight kids, including himself, but had succeeded in getting them to cooperate as well.

Chapter 12

More School Stuff

The next day in gym class, Mr. Gunner was walking through the locker room trying to maintain discipline and get everyone moving in an orderly fashion. He was wearing the same outfit—sweatpants, dress shoes, dress shirt and bow tie.

James Hall, one of the students, stood about two inches taller than Gunner and he knew the kids feared him. James was a good kid, but he was immature for his size. His size drew attention to himself and if he wanted to, he could use it to his advantage to get most anything he desired.

Adam was tying his shoe at his locker, just to the right of James's locker.

Here comes Mr. Gunner, Adam thought to himself. *I wonder what he is going to get into next.* Adam put his head down because he couldn't help smiling at what

A Fighting Chance

funny things could happen now that Gunner was in the room.

"Let's not do so much talking and let's put some speed in our actions," Gunner requested in his goofy voice.

James Hall didn't seem happy and was somewhat annoyed by Gunner's remark. He walked by Gunner and gave him a slap on the back.

"Relax, Little Man," Hall said disrespectfully. "We're hurrying."

Of course, Gunner overemphasized the reaction to the slap and propelled himself into a locker, causing all the kids to laugh, especially Adam.

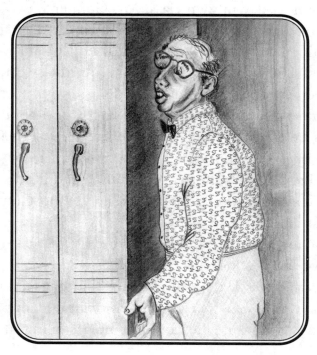

Gunner answered as if nothing were wrong. "That's just great. I love to see enthusiasm."

Hall looked over his shoulder and just shook his head at Gunner. Everything was bothering him and now his locker was stuck, and he couldn't get it open. The handle was jammed and Hall started to bang on his locker in frustration.

"Hey, hey, hey, take it easy. You're going to hurt yourself," Gunner said as he ran over to the locker.

Hall immediately let go of the locker and bent over to tie his shoe. Gunner attempted to open the jammed locker, but didn't succeed. Checking to see if anyone was looking, Gunner slammed his fist into the locker, jarring the handle loose. Hall, along with Adam and the rest of the kids, was startled and quickly looked up to find out what caused the outburst of noise. They all discovered Gunner holding his head as if that was what hit the locker.

"I slipped and hit my head, but the locker is open."

While the kids all found it quite humorous, Adam gave Gunner a smile and a little shake of the head.

In the Gym on the Court

All the kids, both boys and girls, were now out on the court playing basketball. They were having a great time as they ran full court, giving it their best in the scrimmage game they had started.

Poor Mr. Gunner looked like such a klutz. He was

A Fighting Chance

holding a water bottle and a whistle in one hand and a towel and a basketball in the other hand at the same time he was running up and down the court with the kids. Mr. Edwards stood on the sidelines, laughing at this sight.

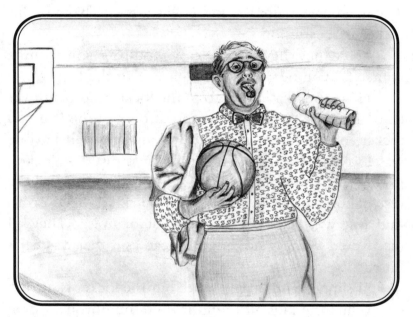

The game was going well and one of the kids passed the ball to James Hall. It hit him on the head by accident. James became very angry and went over to the kid who threw the ball. He pushed him, picking a fight. The kid was scared of James and what might happen next.

"James, I'm sorry, man. Chill out," the kid said in total fear.

James pushed the kid again. "Don't tell me to chill. Watch where you are throwing the ball, Bud."

Gunner stood there watching the boys heat up when Mr. Edwards stepped in.

"All right James, you just bought yourself a three-day suspension."

"For what?" James added, still steaming.

Still holding all the gear, Gunner decided to step in to see if he could help. He could see James's anger and realized that the suspension would cause even greater anger. The problem that caused the anger would still be there.

"Excuse me, please! Excuse me, please! Thank you. Mr. Edwards, with your permission, I would like to have a few words with Mr. Hall and see if we can iron out that suspension. May I?"

Mr. Edwards was not very happy with Gunner's request, but since he was put on the spot with all the other kids looking, he agreed. He looked angrily at both Hall and Gunner.

"You're lucky this time, Mr. Hall!"

Joseph Gunner put his arm around the kid and they headed toward the locker room office.

"You just come with Uncle Joseph and we'll see what we can do for you."

Mr. Edwards watched with anger as they walked off. He didn't like what was going on at all. He wanted Gunner to stick together with him on issues and not try to be the hero that saves the day.

A Fighting Chance

Mr. Edwards told the kids to resume the game that was already in progress, while Mr. Gunner led Hall straight into the office. They both sat down to discuss the situation. Even though Gunner was talking in his nerdy voice, he still had a lot of compassion.

"In the last fifteen minutes, I have experienced two radiant outbursts from you. Now, I don't want to spend a lot of time discussing this matter. However, if you want to keep yourself from a three-day suspension, I suggest you cough up the truth, and I mean the truth...now!"

Hall just sat there for a moment and thought about what he was going to say to Mr. Gunner. Almost in tears, he began to spill his guts.

"I got into an argument with my mother today. I smarted off to her and both of my parents grounded me for a week. I was supposed to go camping this weekend and now I can't. Every time I think about it, it makes me mad and I get carried away."

Gunner interrupted and tried to comfort James with a bit of knowledge.

"You have to learn one thing in life, and that is if you choose to do the wrong thing, you will receive some sort of punishment. What your parents are trying to do is stop this problem before your *little* wrong things turn into *big* wrong things. You may be grounded now, but if you don't learn to control your temper and do the right things, you may find yourself grounded for more than one week. I'm talking prison or even worse…dead. I know it sounds harsh, but that could happen. Now you don't want that, do you?"

Hall sniffed and wiped his eyes as he shook his head, answering Gunner respectfully.

"Now go out there and apologize to that young man. Finish your punishment at home and don't make that mistake again. If you go home with a suspension, you'll be grounded for more than a week."

Hall was so touched by Mr. Gunner's way of putting things. No one had ever taken the time like that before. He just needed to be calmed down so that he could hear the truth and understand it. By this being handled gently, it helped him to make the right decision, rather than fueling his anger even more.

"Mr. Gunner," Hall said, lifting his head, "Thank you and sorry for slapping you on the back earlier."

Gunner, trying to act all cool, replied, "That's quite all right, Son. That's quite all right."

Chapter 13

The Kids Let Gunner in on the Plan

The seven kids were in study hall getting themselves organized. Dominique took this opportunity to talk with her dad, while the other kids gathered in a small group. The bell rang as Adam wheeled in a big cart that was covered with a sheet. He never liked to expose what he was doing until he first had a chance to explain it. Adam also liked the shock it created in others. It made him feel important when he could display a project that made no sense to anyone. He enjoyed the moment as everyone waited to hear what he had to say. Adam drew in their curiosity so deeply that it caused them to listen intently to everything he had to say. By doing this, he realized they might not understand everything, but they would hear it all, which could give them the opportunity to gain knowledge.

As in all people, every one of these eight kids had a very special gift inside of them, but most of the time, people just judged what they saw on the outside. Gunner watched all the kids, including his daughter, gather around the cart to wait for the uncovering of Adam's surprise.

A smile appeared on Gunner's face as he realized that if kids always judged each other by what they saw on the outside, then they would never be known for what they had on the inside. Kind of like Adam and the way the kids used to feel about him by the way he looked. Now it was altogether different.

Gunner realized that if this whole situation had never come up, then none of these kids would ever have taken an interest in Adam. Gunner thought to himself, What a great opportunity to nurture the gifts of these kids and watch them all work together for good. Gunner seemed to be in a trance when he was suddenly interrupted by Adam's boisterous invitation.

"Come on over, Mr. Gunner. Look at the stuff we brought to school today." Even though Adam had invented everything, he included all of his friends who would be a great part in helping all of this to actually work.

Gunner smiled with confidence as he made his way over to the covered cart. He was determined to accept whatever these kids had to offer. He was willing to take whatever ideas they had and work them into his plan to give them a sense of hope and encouragement. Of course, he was keeping in mind that he wouldn't allow any of this to endanger them in any way. Gunner began to realize that what these kids were about to uncover could change the lives of millions everywhere. This was probably just one of many ideas that Adam would introduce to this group. With Adam's inventions and Gunner's wisdom, along with the other seven kids' talents, things could take quite a twist.

Adam gave Mr. Gunner a look of pride and unveiled the materials. He revealed a television monitor, two cell-like phones, radio material, a computer, an enclosed case with little devices in it, and a prototype watch with a screen. Adam realized that the study hall class was only an hour long, so he didn't wait for clearance from Mr. Gunner. He immediately began giving orders to set up shop.

"Billy, hook this line on. Josh, take these antennas and set them up, at least fifteen feet from the base unit."

A Fighting Chance

"Will someone please tell me what is going on?" Gunner asked.

"In a minute, Mr. Gunner," Adam respectfully replied as he continued. "DJ, carefully open this case of earpieces and begin the test pattern I showed you last night. Jackie, I need incoming and outgoing frequencies to be activated upon immediate response. Yuri, your job is to monitor the power increase units when needed. You must not allow the red light to go on, or it will be too late. Dominique, all power units are filtered through this unit. If Yuri's unit cannot increase more power at the time of diffusion, you must increase it manually from sectors three and four. Kelly, you stay with me and feed me all the readouts as they come in.

If we all work together, we can get this job done."

"What job?" Gunner asked with confusion, yet still very impressed.

"Oh yeah," Adam responded to Mr. Gunner, "this is where you come in. My scanning probe is showing that for the last two days, locker number thirty-two, occupied by Ryles McKenzie, has had several different types and weights of drugs filter through it. The drugs we picked up in his locker are the very same drugs that are showing up in several lockers around school."

That explains why he meets that car every day, Gunner thought. He said, "Okay, so what does all of this do?"

Adam proudly explained. "This will help you accomplish what you want to do: Get to the problem before it happens or, in this case, get this kid before he gets busted. Place this in your ear, please, Mr. Gunner."

"Place what in my ear?" Gunner asked, seeing nothing in Adam's hand. He looked closely at Adam's finger and saw something the size of a pinhead. He could hardly see it.

Adam realized that he'd better explain. "It's skin-colored and the size of a tiny dot. However, it will allow you to hear everything we are saying to you. You just place it anywhere on your ear, inside or out—it doesn't matter. It will adhere to your skin and will not come off, no matter what, unless I release it with this switch. Here is a watch for you. It's a prototype. It will allow you to speak to us and, if it works, you will be able to see various information that may aid you in your quest. We can also receive video reception from the watch. If there is something you need us to see, just point the watch at it, and we will see it as clearly as you do. We can even zoom in. Oh, and by the way, it's also in color. F.Y.I., if you have the earpiece in, we are able to pick up your voice as well. If you don't have the earpiece in, then you must use the watch for verbal communication."

Gunner could not believe what he was seeing, but he had to stay composed to maintain control of this operation.

Handing him a cell phone type of device, Adam continued.

"This is a two-way telephone. You can speak to us anywhere in the United States or around the world. No one else can tap in to our conversation either. At the same time, you can program it to connect to your precinct, or you can hit this little button, and it becomes a regular cell phone. I don't recommend that you use it as a cell phone, because it will get charged to my parents, and I'll get in trouble for that."

Gunner chuckled, having just witnessed the child that was still inside this genius. Adam pulled out another tiny little device.

"This little device will fit in the woven material of your bow tie."

"What is it?" Gunner asked.

With a smile, Adam explained, "It's a video camera so that we can see everything you see...and everything you can't since it also has a beaming laser that shoots to an active satellite which can display a photo from space and zoom as close as the hairs in your nose if we want. It's a simple device I invented that will allow the camera to penetrate through steel, brick, or whatever is in its way. It's done by a magnetic X ray which…well, I'll tell you about that later."

"Hold on, Mr. Gunner, there is more," Billy added as Adam pulled out a satellite dish the size of a small dinner plate.

Adam explained, "This plate will allow us to find any documented information recorded anywhere on the face of the earth. When we hear you speak, we can uplink and transmit information to you, within seconds, that may be vital to whatever you are doing. You'll hear it through your earpiece, and you repeat what you have heard, as if you had thought of it yourself. You know, like the news does."

"That's great!" Mr. Gunner replied. "We don't even have this kind of stuff at the precinct. This is all beyond great, but I can't get you guys involved. It could get too dangerous."

"He didn't hear what we just said, did he, Gang?" Billy commented, then continued. "We stay at the base. You go and do all the dangerous work."

There was a pause. Not a word was said. Gunner was thinking and the kids were holding their breath waiting to hear what Gunner would say to all of this.

Gunner wrestled with the fact that they were just

kids, and they shouldn't be involved with stuff like this. But then he remembered that this kind of technology was not available at the precinct...or anywhere else for that matter. "Okay, we'll give it a try."

The kids began to cheer as if their home team just won the Super Bowl.

Gunner broke up their excitement. "Okay. What are we going to say if Miss Ward comes by? She will want to know where Mr. Gunner is."

Adam was prepared for any questions Gunner had. "We can do anything. We can call someone out of class, or we can set off a smoke detector without using smoke. We can defuse her. Don't you worry."

Gunner just nodded his head, accepting everything they were saying. For some reason, Gunner believed this could work.

"Let's do it then!" Gunner said with great excitement.

Adam wasted no time. "Team, man your positions. Mr. Gunner, here, put these glasses on, and use this ink to mark the lockers we spot with drugs in them."

Chapter 14

The Mission Begins

Remaining in his quirky character, Joseph Gunner made his way down the school hallway, which was marked in history as the team's "first mission."

Adam and the rest of the gang were back in study hall running the operation from the main base station. Gunner heard Adam come through loud and clear on the tiny pin-sized earpiece that he placed in his ear.

"Mr. Gunner, can you hear us?" Adam asked with a totally professional tone.

"Yes, loud and clear," Gunner replied in his zany voice.

Adam looked over at Dominique, his forehead all wrinkled. "Does he always sound that dorky?"

"I heard that!" Gunner said surprisingly as his voice came through the speaker at the base station.

Adam realized that Kelly still had the button down

which allowed Adam to communicate with Gunner. Respectfully, Adam reached over and pulled Kelly's hand off the switch. "You have to take your hand off the switch when I'm done responding, Kelly."

"Sorry," Kelly replied. She gave Adam a cutesy look, knowing she made a little mistake.

Just in case anyone might suspect something, Gunner remained in character as he walked down the hall. He could hear Adam's voice as it came through the earpiece.

"Stop! Mr. Gunner, mark locker number twenty-eight. Okay. Keep going. Okay, stop. Mark number thirty-five and forty-eight."

Even though Gunner was using his nerdy character, he still had to discreetly mark the lockers, just in case anyone was looking.

Back in the classroom, Adam grabbed his hair with his hands, as many scientists do. He was getting a readout and needed Billy to investigate it further.

Adam had set up this portable laboratory and knew every function and its ability to produce what he needed it to do.

"Whooe! This is wild!" Adam said, alerting the rest that he was onto something. "Billy, give me a readout as to how many times Ryles was paged in the last two days between the hours of nine A.M. and three P.M."

Billy immediately got to work responding to Adam's request. "Twice yesterday and once the day before."

Adam was on track, but he needed the specifics. "Give me the exact times."

Billy ran his fingers across the computer screen and located what Adam was requesting. "The first day was 11:36 A.M. and the others were 1:06 P.M. and 2:17 P.M."

"Bingo!" Adam said, showing that his suspicion was correct. He continued, "Every time his pager went off, the code 1-2-7 was put in and my heat sensor states that he would make a trip to his locker. Did you catch that, Mr. Gunner?"

"Loud and clear," Gunner replied in his normal voice.

Mr. Gunner had an idea and gave his first order to the team. The more he saw what Adam's inventions could do and how the team worked together, the more he would expand on his ideas. "Page Ryles, Adam. I want to talk to him," Gunner directed in his normal voice.

Nobody on the team moved unless Adam gave the order. It looked like they had been doing this together for years, but the real reason for this was so they wouldn't touch anything that they didn't know about. They didn't want to mess it up.

"Kelly, page this number and put in the code 1-2-7," Adam said.

"Cool, I've got something to do besides switching this little button," Kelly said, as she intently began to dial the phone.

Adam shook his head at the way Kelly was. He

would like to address her cutesy attitude differently, but it would have to be another time. Now, there was work to be done. Adam was always thinking ahead. His mind never stopped.

"Billy, pull up Ryles's locker combination."

Billy loved the computer and was willing to serve Adam in any way he could. He retrieved the information and gave Adam the numbers: 12-7-15. Just as Adam received the combination, Gunner was clearly heard over the portable sound system.

"Adam, get me Ryles's locker combination."

Adam had been thinking ahead and was ready not only to deliver the combination, but to impress Mr. Gunner with their teamwork.

"12-7-15. Did you copy, Sir?"

"That's good, Adam. That's real good."

"Thank you, sir. The page has been sent and Ryles will be on his way soon, according to my predictions."

"Copy, Adam. Keep up the great work," Gunner encouraged them in his normal voice.

The team was working hard at their stations when a red light went off, accompanied by an alarm sound. It wasn't very loud, due to the fact that they were in a classroom, but it did startle the crew.

"What is that?" Dominique asked with concern.

Adam pushed a series of buttons. All the others began to get restless while Adam stayed calm and in control. "Everyone, just relax. It's Mrs. Rossenheimer coming down the hallway. Billy, set off the smoke alarm tester in the west wing."

"Smoke alarm tester?" Billy said, totally confused.

"C-colon-space-4432," Adam said, rattling off the code he devised to set off the alarm tester. "The testing device will draw attention to the smoke alarm without having to evacuate the entire school."

"Oh yeah, that's right. Your mind is like a computer," Billy added, very impressed with Adam's ability to remember everything.

In a moment, after Billy hit the command numbers Adam gave him, the beep that accompanied the red warning light on Adam's computer grew softer and softer as Mrs. Rossenheimer moved away from the study hall class.

"That takes care of her. Kelly, give me a reading on the Gunner satellite scope," Adam said as he continued with the project.

No one responded. Adam thought they had forgotten what the satellite scope was. "What are you guys doing? The satellite scope! You know, the thing in his bow tie!"

Still there was silence. "What's the matter with you guys?"

They all just looked at Adam. No one broke the silence until DJ finally spoke up to ease the curiosity that was all over Adam's face.

"It really worked! I can't believe it!" They all began to boast with excitement and enthusiasm.

"Everything is really working! I mean,

everything!" DJ shouted with amazement.

"Hello. Come back to earth, Team. I need you guys. None of this stuff is any good if the team doesn't man it. Now Kelly, can you give me a reading on the satellite scope?"

Kelly turned the knob, and the satellite scope monitor showed that there was nothing in sight. "All clear," she replied.

"Josh, give me a reading for the area heat sensor control."

"Forty-eight degrees, southeast," Josh answered Adam in his most professional voice.

"Mr. Gunner, Ryles will be turning the corner in about five seconds."

"Copy," Gunner replied.

Gunner took a pen from his pocket and dropped it on the ground to cause a distraction until Ryles came around the corner. At this same time, Ryles showed up and noticed Gunner bent over. But without hesitation, he went on about his business down the hall. That's when Gunner blurted out zanily, "Excuse me, Ryles, can you help me find my pen cartridge?"

Ryles then said, "Right now? Ah, yeah, sure." He couldn't help but think about getting back to his locker with hopes that Gunner didn't question him.

"So, what brings you to these empty hallways?" Gunner asked.

"I'm on my way to the bathroom," Ryles answered, thinking fast.

"Why are you coming all the way over here to use this bathroom?"

"I need to get something out of my locker."

"Could it be this?" Gunner said as he held up the two bags of drugs that he got out of Ryles's locker.

Back in the classroom, Adam and Kelly were watching the monitor intently while all the others awaited instructions from Adam.

"Okay, get ready to go to work. Ryles is shaking."

Dominique took a quick glance around the room. She was excited and nervous at the same time. She couldn't believe she was part of this mission that her dad was in charge of. She realized the job was serious and focused back on the monitor, waiting for direction from Adam.

Gunner didn't say a word. Ryles was speechless. Dead silence filled the hallway, and the eight kids listened to see who would break the silence.

"Where did you find that?" Ryles said as he swallowed the lump in his throat.

"In your locker."

"Who put it there?" Ryles said, seeing if Gunner would buy the lie.

"I believe you did," Gunner replied in his nasally voice.

Ryles began to panic and his head turned back and forth as if he were looking for answers. His panic worsened and he grabbed Mr. Gunner by the shirt and pushed him against the locker. Gunner went along with him because he didn't want to blow his cover.

"You breathe a word of this to anyone and I'll hurt you bad, Nerd Man."

Gunner's shirt was all messed up and his glasses were crooked and way down on his nose. He looked like a pitiful, helpless little man who was at the mercy of the bad man. He reacted with complete self-control, just listening while Ryles pinned him against the locker.

"Ryles, I don't believe you are in any position to be giving orders. Not only have I uncovered drugs in your locker, but I believe they can also be found in—"

That was Adam's cue to feed Gunner the needed information. Adam caught the verbal signal from Gunner and scrambled to get the other locker numbers.

Without a doubt, Adam was successful within a matter of seconds and delivered the information to Mr. Gunner.

"Twenty-eight, thirty-five and forty-eight," Adam said with a voice of accomplishment.

Gunner repeated this to Ryles without missing a beat. "Lockers twenty-eight, thirty-five and forty-eight. Would you like to check them out with me?"

Ryles slowly let go of Mr. Gunner's shirt and put his head down. He spoke in a shaky voice, about to cry. "Are you going to have me arrested?"

"That's not why I'm here."

"I heard you kept Hall from getting suspended. Why?"

"Hall's situation was one thing, but yours is

another. Yours is called drug trafficking and you can be put away for a long time for that. Is that what you want?"

"No. Are you going to tell my aunt?"

Even though Gunner was asking the same questions a detective would ask, they sounded less harsh because of his nerdy voice.

"I want to know who your suppliers are. The car you sometimes meet before and sometimes after school?"

"That's not a supplier. That's my cousin Ashton," Ryles said, trying to throw Gunner off.

Adam didn't buy that comment either. "Ashton...Ashton. Give me the status on him, Billy," Adam instructed.

Billy, punching away at the keys, pulled up the information Adam had requested. "His cousin Ashton is seven months old and lives in North Dakota."

Gunner picked up on that immediately and delivered the information to the ever-lying Ryles.

"Your cousin Ashton is seven months old and lives in North Dakota. Why are you doing this? Maybe we need to get the others here with us. Will they come to your locker if we page them?"

Ryles knew he was caught in every direction. He just nodded his head.

"We're on it, Mr. Gunner. What's the code number?" Adam asked.

Gunner asked Ryles the code and Ryles made him

aware that the code was the same for all of them.

Ryles was so nervous that he didn't even ask Gunner how he knew all of this information.

Adam was working his team back in the classroom. Everyone was serious about their position, no matter what they were doing.

Adam began the process. "Same code. Connely Styles, Dwayne Hines and Lydia Kent. Hit A-3, and it will dial all three at once.

Kelly wasted no time and punched the number immediately, signaling Adam when she was done.

"Okay, Mr. Gunner, they are on their way," Adam relayed, calling Kelly simultaneously.

"Kelly, get me a heat sensor report on all hallway movement."

"Josh, what's your reading?" Kelly said to Josh.

Josh answered seriously, not missing a beat. "Lydia Kent and Connely Styles are on their way. Wait a minute, Dwayne Hines has just entered the hallway."

"Nod your head if you copied that, Mr. Gunner," Adam said, understanding that if Gunner spoke then, Ryles would know that he was wired somehow.

Gunner nodded his head, making it look as if he were just thinking about the whole situation. "Keep your eyes on that corner," Gunner said to Ryles.

Adam started counting down, 10, 9, 8, and so on until the three students turned the corner. At the end of the countdown, Gunner spoke.

"Here they come."

"How did you do that?"

Still in character, Gunner answered, "Don't worry about how, I just know. Come here, you three." He called out to the students, who were walking closer to him, slightly apprehensive.

Adam began to tap his finger on the desk, just thinking and anticipating his next move.

After a moment, he rapped his hand on the desk, knowing what to do.

"Billy, pull up all the information you can get on all four of them, starting with Ryles. I need family backgrounds and anything else you can think of. As it comes up, save it and transfer it to Kelly's mobile unit."

"Right away, Adam," Billy answered.

Billy had no problem locating the information Adam requested. As the information came up, both Adam and Kelly could hear the beeping of Kelly's mobile keypad. Her keypad was a very small computer that hung from a belt around her waist. Adam got it from the grocery store. It was a gadget that stores use to do their inventory. With a little tweaking, Adam had turned it into a fully working computer.

"Hey, Adam, I've got information coming up on my screen about Ryles McKenzie," Kelly said.

"Read it to me."

Kelly then read the news aloud in a very professional manner. "Jonathan McKenzie, brother, age fifteen, has been locked up in juvenile detention for twenty-two months for the sale and possession of drugs, primarily cocaine. The record shows that his supplier, eighteen-year-old Rodney Guston, who is serving no time, blew the whistle on him."

Adam had an idea: "I bet Rodney Guston is the same supplier who framed Jonathan. Mr. Gunner, if you copy all of this information, hit the top right corner of your watch. If you want these stats read back to you, push the lower left corner of your watch and, if it works, all the information along with a picture will appear on your watch screen. Keep in mind, I am still in the developing stages with this watch."

"Gunner is pushing the lower left corner. He wants the information," Kelly anxiously commented.

Adam punched the information through and waited a moment to see if it worked. All the kids were gathered around the monitor with anticipation.

"Yes! It worked!" Adam was pleased to say.

Gunner took a moment to review the stats that had been transmitted through to his watch.

"Now, I'm going to ask you all a question and I expect the truth. Do you know a man named Rodney Guston?" Gunner asked. He waited for the answer with his finger to his chin in his goofy style.

All four students looked at each other, not knowing what to say. Ryles spoke up, "Umm. No, we don't know a Rodney."

At this point, Yuri was picking up Miss Ward on the satellite scope.

"Miss Ward is at twenty degrees south."

Dominique began to express slight panic. "Oh my gosh, now what are we going to do? She's so close. Do something, Adam!"

"Relax, Dominique. What do you think we have all of this stuff for? Billy, set off a tester alarm in the north wing before Dominique chews off her entire finger."

Billy hit the button and the alarm sounded. He turned to Dominique and smirked.

"I wasn't worried, Billy. I knew you could handle it."

DJ threw a piece of wadded paper at Dominique for being so goofy. Without even looking away from his monitor, Josh nonchalantly told DJ to pick it up.

DJ answered in a respectful but funny way, "Right. Sorry, Josh."

The alarm was going off, but Miss Ward didn't seem to notice it. She just focused on Mr. Gunner and the four students standing in the hallway. By the look on her face, she assumed that, whatever the problem was, Gunner most likely caused it. But to remain professional in front of the students, she held her abrasive tongue.

"Mr. Gunner, is everything all right?—"

Miss Ward was interrupted by Mrs. Rossenheimer on the walkie-talkie, "Miss Ward, you are needed immediately in the north wing. Another smoke tester is malfunctioning."

"Thank you, Mrs. Rossenheimer. I'll be right there. Mr. Gunner, take care of this problem here and get these students back to their classrooms."

"Yes, Miss Ward. Right away," Gunner said, saluting Miss Ward. He quickly turned back to the foursome. "Again, I'm going to ask you. Do you know Rodney Guston?"

"Again, I am going to answer...no!" Ryles said, standing his ground.

Gunner was forced to divulge information that might hurt Ryles.

"Just so you know, Ryles, your brother, Jonathan, was not busted because he did the crime. He was busted because he was framed and set up by this Rodney guy. Why was he framed? Because Rodney wanted to shove the blame on your brother so the attention would be taken off of him. This puts closure in the books, and the so-called heat is off the subject. Rodney can continue his street work.

"Your brother is serving time for a crime he definitely committed, but he was arrested and put in prison because of Rodney. It was Guston who framed him and got him involved with drug trafficking in the first place. Your brother didn't want to have anything to do with it, but he was forced to, out of fear, into selling drugs for Rodney. One thing led to another, and before Jonathan knew it, he was deep into a life of crime.

"Now I don't believe any of you want to begin a life of crime. I don't want to have you arrested. I want you to help me get this Rodney fellow off the streets, and to see your lives make their way on the right road. Now I'll be quiet and you take it from here."

After a moment passed, Ryles finally spoke up, "Rodney's our man."

"What are you doing?" Connely, one of the other boys, said to Ryles. "How do you know what he said about your brother is true?"

Adam figured out the answer to that question long before it was even asked, "Mr. Gunner, use the phone and hit the send button. We're dialing in the detention center where Jonathan is. We're telling them Detective Galardi is requesting to speak to Jonathan McKenzie. Continue to speak in your goofy voice. We have a voice enhancer patched in. It will make your voice sound normal."

Gunner heard everything Adam instructed and he continued with the four students.

"I'm going to need more answers. So in order for you to believe me, let's just give your brother a call."

Gunner pushed the button on the phone and waited as it rang. The four kids were so into what was going on that they didn't even question how Gunner, the weirdo that he was, could have all of this information about them.

"Hello," Gunner said, surprised that it was answered so quickly.

"This is Officer Latsky, Detective Galardi. We've been expecting your call. Let me put Jonathan on the line."

"Thank you. I'll wait," Gunner said, nodding his head.

"Hello," said Jonathan.

Gunner continued, "Jonathan, my name is Mr. Gunner. I have your brother here, and I would like you to pass along some very important information to him, or he will end up in the same place you are or maybe even worse. Tell him about Rodney Guston."

"Hurry, take the voice enhancer off so Ryles can talk and it won't sound weird," Billy said to Adam.

"Don't worry, it only kicks on when it hears Mr. Gunner's voice. Haven't you guys figured me out yet?" Adam said with a smile.

There was a change in Ryles's expression as he reached for the phone. He didn't believe that his brother was on the other end. He grabbed the phone from Mr. Gunner with a cocky attitude.

"All right, who is this?" Ryles asked, not expecting to hear Jonathan's voice. He changed the way he felt almost immediately. His mouth hung open, and he just listened. After a few moments a tear rolled down Ryles's face. "I will, I promise. I miss you too, Jonathan. Bye."

Ryles slowly handed the phone back to Mr. Gunner. Next, Ryles spoke humbly, "You were right. My brother said to do whatever you tell me to do."

"I want you to call Rodney right now and tell him that you can't continue doing business with him. Tell him that you will meet him after school at the far end of the property to inform him you will not be involved with him anymore. Don't worry about a thing, there will be plenty of people to protect you."

While Gunner was telling him all of this, he was also writing out hall passes for the kids in case they got stopped on their way back to class. "Here. These are your excuses for being detained in the hall."

After Gunner handed the students their passes, he

held out his personal cell phone for Ryles to make the call to Rodney. Ryles took the phone and just stared at it for a minute. He didn't really know what to say to Rodney. When Ryles looked up at his friends, he was surprised to see that they all nodded their heads in support of Gunner's request. He just smiled as he realized he was doing the right thing.

"Mr. Gunner, I'm sorry about calling you a nerd."

"That's quite all right. I'm getting used to it. It doesn't bother me at all."

Ryles just smiled and made the call.

Chapter 15

Miss Ward Is Upset

Mr. Gunner stood with his arms outstretched like a scarecrow while Adam removed the wires and equipment from his body. The other seven kids just stared, completely astonished at the events that had just occurred. They beamed with excitement, filled with feelings of self-accomplishment at their successful teamwork.

"So, Dad, we did good, huh?" Dominique asked, sure of his answer.

"No!" Gunner answered abruptly in his normal speaking voice. The faces of the kids just dropped. Their smiles disappeared and the kids remained quiet and motionless, surprised about the comment Gunner just made.

Gunner broke his stern look and cracked a smile. "You did absolutely great!"

A Fighting Chance

There was a sigh of relief from the students. They all started talking at once, reminiscing about the success of their mission.

About this time, the classroom PA system beeped, which usually was a signal from the office to someone in that room.

Everyone, including Mr. Gunner, clammed up, eagerly waiting for someone to speak. To no one's surprise, it was Mrs. Rossenheimer. "Mr. Gunner, Miss Ward would like to see you immediately. Mrs. Rice will be down to watch your class."

Gunner responded in his goofy voice. "Ah, yes, Mrs. Rossenheimer, ma'am. I'll promptly make my way to your office."

"Miss Ward's office, not mine," she added with her seemingly unpleasant attitude.

"Yes, that is correct. It's my mistake. Right away on that mistake," Gunner added just to keep his character going.

"Just get up here now, Mr. Gunner!"

The kids heard the click in the PA system, indicating that she was no longer in communication. The class waited for a second to make sure she was not still on the PA and then burst out laughing.

Gunner settled them down and requested order in the room. "Hurry and get this stuff put away before the Rice lady gets here."

"Roger," Adam said, realizing this was part of the job as well.

"Who's Roger?" Kelly asked, confused.

Adam just shook his head and didn't even bother to explain.

The bell rang and Gunner headed toward the door. "No need for the Rice lady to watch you guys. Class dismissed. Gotta go!"

None of the eight kids left until they finished helping Adam put away the rest of the equipment.

Mr. Gunner walked clumsily out into the hallway where kids were moving to and from their classes. He smiled and waved at all the kids, none of whom were even paying attention to or responding to him.

There were cheerleaders hanging banners on the wall. The janitor was mopping the floor. Another man was on a ladder changing the batteries in a smoke alarm. Gunner laughed to himself, knowing that their little mission with all of Adam's equipment caused complete confusion with all of the electronics in the school. He continued his journey toward the office, completely unaware of a catastrophe of slapstick destruction that started happening just behind him and he had nothing to do with it this time!

Two kids were goofing off and they accidentally bumped into the guy mopping the floor. The mopper lost his balance and knocked over the bucket of soapy water. This caused kids to slip and collide into each other, which resulted in books and junk falling out of their lockers. This domino effect spread to the cheerleaders. The banner ripped and everyone slipped and slid into each other. A group of kids slid right into the man changing the batteries. This man grabbed on to the steel girders and dangled in mid air.

Gunner continued to walk just ahead of all of this, leaving everyone behind him either on the floor or on their way to the floor. Gunner heard it but didn't even want to look back for fear he might get blamed for it.

As Joseph Gunner was just a few steps from the office door, Miss Ward and the ever-crabby Mrs. Rossenheimer stepped into the hallway, looking totally shocked. They both stared at Gunner, thinking that it could be none other but him who caused this big of a mess.

Gunner stepped right up to them. "Yes, Miss Ward, I believe you wanted to see me?"

"What...have...you...done...now,...Mr. Gunner?" Miss Ward said through gritted teeth, trying to contain her anger from exploding in front of the students.

Miss Ward looked directly at the secretary just inside the door. "Get me my bullhorn, please!"

Gunner answered in his silly voice, which just about sent Miss Ward over the edge. "Nothing, Miss Ward. I've done nothing. As you can see, I am in front of this little catastrophe. This chain reaction of events clearly happened behind me, not in front of me. Therefore, note for the record, I stand innocent before those in authority."

Miss Ward leaned over and spoke loudly and directly into his ear, "Shut up, please!"

Gunner became cross-eyed for a moment. "Yes ma'am. Not another word."

Miss Ward put the bullhorn up to her lips and called out, "Students! Students! Quiet, please!"

They settled and she continued. "Is everyone all

right? Is anyone hurt?"

The kids motioned to her that they all were okay. A few of the boys put the ladder back under the dangling man.

Miss Ward continued. "I expect to see all of you in your classes before the bell. Is that understood?" She didn't even wait for an answer. She said it and she expected it to get done.

"Mrs. Rossenheimer, please get to the bottom of this. Mr. Gunner, would you kindly step into my office please?"

"Why thank you, Miss Ward. I appreciate the invitation."

She couldn't believe this guy. Could it get any worse? No matter what she said, Gunner's answer was way out there in left field.

Both Gunner and Miss Ward began walking through the main office to get to her private office. Gunner couldn't just walk and keep his mouth shut. The character he portrayed normally babbled to everyone along the way. No matter who he talked to, they just ignored him and shook their heads.

"Good to see you, Ms. Elridge. It's always a pleasure to see your smiling face in the office. I mean that." She was not smiling. She was gritting her teeth to keep from saying what was really on her mind.

"Hey, great tie, Mr. Walder. You'll have to let me know where you got that. I wonder if they sell it in a bow tie style? That would really go great with one of my outfits."

Miss Ward couldn't get to the door fast enough. She forcefully opened the door and threw her hand up, motioning for Gunner to step inside. He knew she was very upset, but he played it off as if nothing were wrong. He had to remain in character if he wanted to keep his cover. So, he didn't stop talking. "Miss Ward, he is a sharp dresser, that Mr. Walder, you know that? I mean, he really is."

Miss Ward was not paying attention to any word that Gunner said. She was just about to settle in her chair when Gunner shut the door to her office and of course another picture fell off the wall, breaking into pieces.

"I always forget how freely that door moves. Again, I apologize for the picture. I'll be more than happy to replace the frame."

"Mr. Gunner, have a seat."

Gunner sat carefully in the seat, crossing his legs and folding his hands in his lap. He gave Miss Ward his complete attention. She questioned him about the situation concerning the four students in the hallway earlier.

"The teachers of those students contacted my office and informed me that their students did not return to their classes for fifteen or twenty minutes. Now, I saw you detaining them myself. Whatever for, Mr. Gunner?"

A Fighting Chance

"I just wanted to apologize to your nephew for opening the door on him the other day."

"Mr. Gunner, that doesn't take fifteen minutes. But you know what? I don't even want to hear the rest. I'm not interested. However, I do want to make one thing clear. I don't want to see you near my nephew again. Is that perfectly clear?"

Gunner tried to answer again, but Miss Ward stopped him.

"Just nod your head. Please don't speak."

Gunner nodded his head as she asked. Miss Ward took a moment to contemplate how she was going to say what she needed to tell Gunner next. She decided there was only one way and that was to just say it.

"Mr. Gunner, this school needs to replace you, but my hands are tied since, according to the school board, there are no replacements for you at this time. I don't know what you said to them, but they will not release you from this school. Does someone in your family have a high position at the school board? Is that what it is?"

She really didn't ask the question expecting Gunner to answer her, but he felt it was necessary to explain.

"No, my family doesn't even live in this state, Miss Ward, although many of them are considering moving to this area because of the climate and—"

"Mr. Gunner! Please!"

He immediately stopped talking and just stared with a goofy, annoying look on his face.

"Thank you. I'm asking you to please take a month or less to find yourself another job and resign. Do you think you can do that? Just answer me without talking and shake your head, yes or no."

Gunner gave a slightly positive, apprehensive nod, and Miss Ward continued.

"That's just wonderful. Thank you so much, Mr. Gunner. That will be all."

Gunner got up to leave and Miss Ward stood as well.

"I'll get the door for you, Mr. Gunner, and please don't touch anything."

"Why, thank you—"

Miss Ward interrupted him before he could go on rambling. "And don't say another word either!"

"I—"

"No, no, Mr. Gunner. That's talking. Shhh." She put her finger over her lips and smiled as Gunner walked on down the hall.

Chapter 16

Meeting at Gunner's House

The bell rang, signaling the end of the school day. Mr. Gunner and the eight kids made their way out the front doors of the school to the bus pickup area.

As in any school, kids are kids, and when the thinking part of the day is over the fun begins. But not for the crew Gunner had walking with him. They seemed to live and breathe this new venture that had come their way.

Gunner stopped abruptly and squinted his eyes to see who was running toward him. He realized that it was Ryles McKenzie.

"Hey, You Guys. Give me a minute alone with this kid," Gunner said in his normal voice to the eight kids as Ryles came closer.

A Fighting Chance

"Mr. Gunner," Ryles said, putting his hands on his knees while trying to catch his breath. He continued, "Rodney contacted me back and said he wanted me to take a few weeks to change my mind. He said he was confident that I would make the right decision."

Gunner was back in full character as he answered, "Okay, take the time he suggested, but when he calls you to meet, contact me immediately. Is that understood?"

"Yes, sir. My brother told me to do everything you tell me to do."

"Great. Not a word of this to anybody," Gunner said, pointing his finger in a seriously nerdy way.

After reaffirming that his lips were sealed, Ryles took off.

Then the kids gathered around Gunner, curiously wondering what Ryles said.

Gunner gave them further instruction.

"I need to talk to all of you and fill you in on some important rules. Why don't you all have your parents bring you to my house for pizza tonight and give me a chance to meet them, too? Don't mention anything about all of this stuff, just inform them that the teacher has just called a meeting. Okay? Have all of you got that?" They all responded positively.

"Good. I'll take care of the rest. Be at my house at 6:30 p.m. Does everyone know where I live?"

They all said, "Yes," making it obvious to Gunner that they had made each other aware of all the important points. Gunner was amazed at what was happening with these kids. Men and women go to school for years to gain this sort of knowledge and teamwork.

As Gunner watched them all leave, he shook his head, still stunned and amazed at the willingness and teamwork flowing from the group! A quick glance to the left allowed Gunner to see Miss Ward out of the corner of his eye. He put his head down and darted in the opposite direction. I don't need any more trouble from her, he thought to himself.

The Meeting Begins

It was 6:25 P.M. and many of the kids were already at Gunner's house. DJ, Dominique, Billy, Jackie, Adam, and Yuri were all in the backyard with Gunner planning a goofy game of touch football. A few of the parents filtered back there to mingle with each other and become better acquainted.

Adam was sitting over to the side watching them have a good time. Football was not his thing, but that didn't stop him from enjoying himself as he watched his new friends go at it. They decided to pair off, organize teams, and have a little scrimmage until Mr. Gunner said it was time to stop.

Gunner motioned to the kids to hang on a minute while he went to answer the front door, since his wife, Monica, was busy in the kitchen. Kelly was ringing the doorbell and peeking in the window.

A Fighting Chance

Gunner opened the door for Kelly and her parents. Kelly just stared at Gunner in surprise. "Oh, I'm sorry, I must be at the wrong house," Kelly said.

"No, you aren't, Kelly. Come in," Gunner said.

"Is that you, Mr. Gunner? Oh my gosh! He doesn't look like that in school," Kelly told her parents.

Kelly stared again. Not only was Mr. Gunner in normal clothes, he didn't have his funny teeth in, and he was not wearing glasses. And what really threw her off in the first place was that he wasn't bald anymore. He had a full head of hair!

"You were like wearing a bald wig or something?"

"Yes, Kelly. It's all part of the job. Let's go in, shall we?"

Gunner introduced himself to her parents and told them to make themselves at home. "We are going to play a quick game of touch football. Grab a soft drink, and we'll get started in just a moment."

Gunner went back outside, ready to join the game. The lineup was Billy, DJ and Yuri against Dominique, Jackie and Mr. Gunner. Dominique was touching up her hair, saying, "I still can't figure out how to play this game."

Mr. Gunner explained very simply, "Dominique, it goes like this…Jackie will hike me the ball. I'll pass it to you, and you pass it to Jackie. Got it?"

"Piece of cake," Dominique said, trying her best not to get messed up. The ball was hiked to Gunner. He passed it to Dominique and she began to panic. She screamed and ran the other way. Jackie was yelling that she was open, but Dominique didn't seem to hear her. All she knew was that Billy, DJ and Yuri were running toward her.

"Stop!" Dominique yelled out, causing them all to stop right in their tracks. "My mom is motioning that she needs help bringing the pizzas out."

The three boys looked at her in total shock that she stopped the game just for that.

"Well, are you going to help her or not?" Dominique said to the boys.

Billy, DJ and Yuri were apologetic and made their way toward the back door of the house.

As soon as they got a few steps away, Dominique took off in the direction of her goal line.

The boys then realized they had been had and they took off running after Dominique. Dominique began to scream and laugh at the same time. The boys were closing in on her and she finally passed the ball to Jackie. Jackie, athlete that she was, had no problem running in for the touchdown.

Jackie spiked the ball and Dominique brushed her hands together like a little Miss Princess.

"Piece of cake," Dominique said. "You just gotta know how to handle boys!"

Gunner shook his head and smiled while the three boys argued that they needed to run that play over and that cheating was definitely up for discussion.

Gunner decided that it was time to get down to

business and led them inside to join the others.

"Everyone, just help yourselves. Eat as much as you'd like. My precinct contacted all of you to meet us here so that you would know everything was legitimate. That's why I didn't have the kids explain anything to you. Anyway, my name is Joseph Galardi, A.K.A. Mr. Gunner, and this is my wife, Monica, and my daughters Dominique, Nicole and Jenna."

Everyone waved and said, "Hi," to the Galardi family as Mr. Gunner continued. "Just call me Mr. Gunner so no one gets confused. We have stumbled upon something unique and I would like to fill you in on it. I need your permission to involve your kids in continuing this great work that has accidentally but successfully begun here."

Mr. Gunner proceeded to tell them how they all met and how Adam's inventions and devices had created teamwork second to none. The parents were very intrigued when Mr. Gunner explained that their mission was to get to those in need before disaster took place at any level. After he explained all of the details, Gunner assured these parents of their kids' safety.

"So, you see, the kids would be the base unit and I would be the field unit. They would not be allowed to act upon anything without consulting with me first. If you agree to all of this, it would remain confidential business and no one, not even family members, would be allowed to know any of this!"

"I think this is a wonderful idea. You can count us in," Adam's father said.

The rest of the parents felt the same. Yuri's father politely asked for permission to speak and added even more to this great plan. "This is great for this case, so why stop here at the school? Why not help the community?"

The others agreed with Yuri's father.

"I don't know about that," Gunner added. "I really hadn't given the idea much thought. Some details would have to be worked out, but it sounds great. It's true, you know, why stop at one case? I think that we should go as far as this can take us. I don't know how I can move from one place to another so quickly, but I'm sure we'll figure it out."

"Mr. Gunner," Adam said while raising his hand.

"Yes, Adam, it's not necessary to raise your hand. We're not in school at the moment."

"Oh, sorry." Adam continued, "Can you and The Fighting Chance Team meet me at my house tomorrow?"

"The who?" Billy asked.

"No, The Who was a band in the seventies. The Fighting Chance Team is what I said. We're a team, and Mr. Gunner wants to give kids a fighting chance rather than just put them away and let the prison system raise them."

"Cool name," Billy remarked.

"Yeah, that is a great name! Tomorrow will be fine," Mr. Gunner said, agreeing with Adam's request.

The rest of the kids agreed excitedly, wondering what Adam had up his sleeve this time!

"That is, if it's okay with you, Mom and Dad?" Adam asked respectfully.

"Of course it's okay, Honey. Anything we can do to help out," Adam's mom enthusiastically replied.

Chapter 17

Adam Reveals the Invention of Inventions

Once again, the gym class was left in Mr. Gunner's hands. The boys and girls were out of control. They had taken Gunner's bow tie and wouldn't give it back to him.

Billy and Adam were sitting on the sidelines laughing because they knew Gunner was putting on a really great act.

This game of keep away was interrupted when Josh ran up to Mr. Gunner and handed him a note, filling him in on the details. "I was on my way back to the office when I saw that your car had four flat tires and this note was on your windshield. I gotta get back to the office. They are waiting for me."

"Thank you," Gunner said in his normal voice but still acting really goofy with the other kids.

A Fighting Chance

"Hey, don't say anything to them in the office about my tires. I'll just tell them I ran over a bunch of nails or something."

Gunner read the note. It said, "Stay out of our business, Nerd Man!" Gunner tucked it into his shirt pocket and continued chasing after his bow tie.

Out of the corner of his eye, Gunner spotted Mr. Edwards entering the gym. Then he really poured on the goofiness. The kids ran up in the bleachers and Gunner chased after them. After taking only one step up the bleachers, he tripped and fell to the ground, causing laughter to break out all over the gym.

Mr. Edwards ran to rescue Gunner and blew his whistle. Instantly the kids stopped and looked his way.

"What is going on around here? You know I don't expect this from any of you. Gunner, what's happening here?"

Gunner started rambling in his weird voice. "From my perspective, I feel it was caused from some sort of sugar imbalance. It just caught on like a snow storm with no warning and I couldn't pull it under control, to be honest with you, Sir."

Mr. Edwards just shook his head. He couldn't figure out what planet Gunner was from. He was right on the edge of losing his patience with him when one of the girls explained what happened.

"Andrew took Mr. Gunner's bow tie and everyone started to play keep away."

"Thank you," Mr. Edwards said, gesturing.

"I could see that for myself, Young Lady. Now you can all run laps for the rest of this period and you can thank…" Mr. Edwards caught himself as he looked over at Gunner. "Get moving. Every one of you. Gunner, why don't you run with them?"

"Oh, sure, that would be great. No problem. I always love the chance to get some exercise."

Gunner took off running, but after taking two steps, he fell flat on his face.

Mr. Edwards stared and began to laugh, but then stopped and reminded himself that he was supposed to be angry.

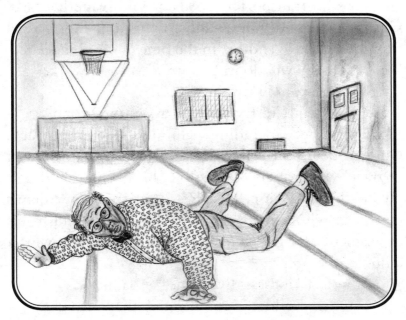

A Fighting Chance

Later That Day

The famous eight along with Mr. Gunner were running down Adam's basement stairs. Adam stopped at the bottom and took a long deep breath. "Are you guys ready?" Adam asked as he led them to a covered object about five feet tall.

They all waited with excitement as Adam uncovered his new invention—some sort of box with doors on it. No one knew what it was. They just stared, waiting for Adam to explain.

Gunner asked, "What is it?"

"It's a transporter," Adam said eagerly. "Mr. Gunner, you said you couldn't figure out how to get from one place to another in the time frame you needed. Well, this baby will do it. You want to see it work?"

They all couldn't wait for this.

"Who wants to try?" Adam asked the group.

Everyone, including Gunner, stepped back. Gunner, being the only one who realized that this sort of travel was virtually impossible, bit his lip. He didn't say anything because he didn't want to crush Adam's creativity. Gunner planned to let Adam finish his experiment and give him the chance to explain why it didn't work later.

"I'm just kidding, Everyone," Adam said.

Gunner nodded, confirming that he knew it wouldn't work. He was about to speak when Adam continued.

"It's only a mock-up. It won't transfer human molecular structure with such low voltage. Kelly, hand me that baseball glove."

Gunner took another step back and crossed his arms. He really wanted to say something, but he figured it best to just stay quiet for a while.

Kelly handed Adam the glove and Adam placed it behind the doors of the box. After closing the doors, he moved over to the control panels.

"There are three sectors here. They all need to be activated at the same time. Dominique, DJ and Jackie, get into your positions in front of the sectors, please," Adam said as he pointed to the three sectors.

Adam picked up a remote control-looking device and started to give more instructions.

"Okay, get ready to activate all sectors, and turn the keys to the right." The keys were about two feet long and made of clear plastic. They were inserted deep into the control panel and were just sticking out, waiting to be turned.

"Okay, ready on three? One...two...three."

They all turned their keys at the same time. Gunner just stood in the corner with a doubtful smile on his face. Adam pushed a button on his control panel. A glowing light came from inside the box. The kids just stared at the box, not knowing what to do next.

Adam smiled as the glowing light from the box disappeared. Nobody said a word. Adam looked at Yuri and motioned for him to open the door.

A Fighting Chance

Yuri went over to the box and carefully opened the double doors.

"Where'd it go?" he asked.

Gunner uncrossed his arms.

"Kelly, go upstairs and open the front door," Adam instructed.

Adam then explained this invention to the group. "I can send the object to wherever I want it to go. I use a magnified longitude and latitude map to pinpoint the exact location, then *whsss*. Away it goes."

Gunner walked closer to them. "This can't be done. It's impossible," he said, not having anything to back up his statement.

"Well, Mr. Gunner," Adam said, "the impossible has just happened."

Kelly came running down the stairs. She stopped halfway down and out of breath. "There was nothing out there."

The other six kids looked totally disappointed while Gunner began to nod his head, affirming the fact that he knew it was impossible.

Adam ignored Kelly's negative comment and held out his hand.

"Hand it over, Kel."

She gave her little cutesy smile and danced down the rest of the stairs, exposing the glove from behind her back. She tossed it to Adam. They all started clapping like it was a dog trick.

"It really worked!" Gunner said with disbelief.

"Of course it worked," Adam replied. He continued with some concern, "My only problem is to find out how to generate the amount of power needed to transport human molecular structure. The wattage and megahertz are mind-boggling."

Josh quickly responded, "Power it by the energy that comes from the sun. Store the power somehow and activate it when needed. That way you won't need to use any kind of nuclear energy."

"Stay out of it, Josh, and let the genius figure it out," Jackie said, giving Josh a little punch on the shoulder.

"He's right," Adam said.

"Like I said, Josh. Help the genius figure it out," Jackie added, changing her tune.

"No, he's really right, Jackie. I can make it work by using a magnified satellite receptor dish with a storage unit to filter in the energy at the push of a button. You're a genius, Josh."

Josh smiled as he raised his hands to welcome his cheers, while everyone patted him on the back.

Gunner noted Adam's serious look. "What's the matter, Adam?"

"We don't have the room to store the unit we have to build. We can all put our heads together and build the unit, but we wouldn't have anywhere to store it. We would probably need about 3,000 square feet."

A Fighting Chance

"We'll find a place. You just start drawing," Gunner said to Adam, knowing that space was their least concern.

"You got it," Adam said as he continued with authority. "Yuri, get your pencil ready."

Chapter 18

The Old Mill

Riding proudly with her hair blowing in the wind as it flew out of the bottom of her helmet, Dominique sported herself on the back of the Harley with her dad in the driver's seat. They pulled off the main road and up a dirt road, heading toward an old mill that had been abandoned for thirty years. Gunner put the kickstand down and powered off the monster-sounding Harley Davidson as both he and Dominique climbed off the bike. Dominique removed her helmet to fix her hair and brushed off the dust from her clothes. Gunner stood there with his hands resting on his hips, staring at the old mill.

A Fighting Chance

Dominique joined up with her dad and looked at the mill as well. "Where are we?" she asked, not seeing anything that she recognized.

"This is where we can store Adam's laboratory."

The mill was filled with junk, and the walls had holes in them. In some areas, large chunks of the wall were missing.

"Dad, no way!" she said, concerned that her dad might be serious.

Gunner began to walk into the old building, and Dominique trailed behind, hoping this was not one of her dad's silly jokes.

They carefully stepped up a board that led from the

ground level to the inside of the mill, since the stairs were broken and the board was the only way in. Gunner helped Dominique up into the mill. She was not thrilled about going into this strange place, but she knew that her father wouldn't lead her wrong.

The two of them made their way through the junk. They came to a pulley-driven elevator that still seemed to work.

"This mill has been vacant for over thirty years. I used to play on this elevator when I was your age. Hop on."

Dominique threw her dad a look that said, "No way!"

"Okay," Gunner said as he lowered himself on the elevator.

Dominique started to freak out, realizing that she was going to be left there by herself. "Oh no, you don't. You're not leaving me up here with these old bug-covered things."

Dominique jumped on as her dad continued to lower them by the pulley system. They reached the bottom and Gunner opened the door. It was dark and Dominique was not a happy camper.

"I can't see anything," she said, hoping her dad would have a solution.

Gunner reached for something outside the elevator. "Hang on for a second," he said. He pulled in an old lantern and wiped off the dust. It still had fuel in it.

"I knew this old lantern would still be here. Some

A Fighting Chance

things never change. No one knows about this old place except a few friends and me, and they all have moved away. The people who own this property haven't lived in it for almost forty years."

He reached around to the back of the lantern, pulled out a match and fired up the lamp. Stepping off the elevator, he moved the lamp around to expose the dark areas, but the lamp didn't make enough light for them to see very well at all.

Dominique looked down at her feet and saw a rat crawling around her shoe. She let out a big scream and scared her dad half out of his skin.

"Daddy, Daddy, Daddy!" she screamed. "Oh my

gosh, oh my gosh. It's a monster!"

Dominique ran around trying to grab onto her dad, spinning him around with her. She finally made it to the back of her dad and jumped on, piggyback style.

"My goodness, Dominique. I'm glad you didn't see the snake over in the corner."

She let out another big scream. "What snake? Which corner?"

Gunner laughed, just teasing her as he continued to look around.

There is dirt and junk everywhere in this place, Dominique thought, still shaking from her experience.

"This place is perfect," Gunner said.

"Yep, it's a real palace, Dad," Dominique replied sarcastically.

"It will be when it's cleaned up."

"Who's going to clean all of this up?"

Gunner just smiled.

A few days later, on Saturday, The Fighting Chance Team was hard at work in the basement of the old mill.

The team had hung spotlights all around the basement so the mess would be much easier to see. A lot of junk and dirt lay cluttered all over the floor. Mr. Gunner and the kids were sweeping and dumping, removing the junk and putting it on the elevator.

While they were all in the middle of cleaning, Billy tapped Kelly on the shoulder. When she turned around she saw that he was holding a dead rat by the tail right in front of her. Of course Kelly screamed so loud that she got everyone's attention. They all started to laugh at her, and she got mad. She started to hit Billy, but he shook the rat in her face again and began to chase her around the basement. Kelly continued to scream and run from Billy, but then he mercifully gave up and threw the rat into the trash.

As the days passed, the basement began to show some progress, but it had a long way to go to be ready for The Fighting Chance Team.

During one clean-up day, Gunner, Adam, Yuri and Billy checked over the blueprints that Yuri came up with based on Adam's directions. Adam approved Yuri's drawings and then motioned to Gunner to make a mark in a specific area of the wall with a piece of chalk. Adam knew the exact measurements where he wanted the mark to be made and if Gunner was a little off, he would just have him erase it and start over again until he marked the right spot.

Adam finally got the mark where he wanted it, realized that it wasn't a good spot after all, and had Mr. Gunner erase it. This went on a couple of times until Gunner finally wrote on the wall "Adam is a really confused kid." He was joking of course, but Adam remained very serious.

Adam didn't understand how Gunner could joke around at a time like this. He thought *Okay, I'll show him*. He picked up his invention that erased chalk, pointed it at what Gunner wrote on the wall, and gave the red button a push. All the chalk dropped to the floor.

Adam smirked at Gunner, showing him that he still had a few tricks of his own.

After three days, the basement was finally cleaned. They were then ready to build the invention to operate the transporter. Gunner and the team used a pulley system to hoist up steel beams into place, one on either side of the door. Two beams would support the pressure caused by the transport. Wood or plastic would not be strong enough because the pressure caused by the amount of energy would snap the beams.

Yuri approached Adam, who was doing some figuring and asked, "What do all those numbers mean?"

"Oh, these? At the time of entry or departure, the transporter sends off too many X rays to be exposing ourselves each time. I'm trying to figure out how we can avoid this. Any suggestions, Mr. Gunner?" Adam asked.

Gunner walked away from helping the boys with the pulley system and remarked, "Why don't you—"

Right about that time, a thought popped into Adam's head, and he cut Mr. Gunner off with his idea.

"We'll just put together a jumpsuit of some kind that is lined with lead and a ball cap the same way. That's the end of that problem."

"Glad I could be of help, Adam," Gunner added, smiling.

"Oh, sorry, Mr. Gunner. Ideas come quickly to me when I'm under pressure."

"My mom can make an outfit in an hour. It won't

be a problem for her at all," Kelly suggested.

Before Adam could say anything, Gunner jumped in.

"Yuri, just draw something that looks cool. I have an image to uphold."

"We can tell," Yuri said, laughing as always. When the other kids began laughing, Yuri started his belly laugh, more than he ever did.

Several days later, Gunner and the team were putting some finishing touches on the control panel, when Kelly and her mother dropped in.

"Hello," Kelly's mom said, as she made her way down the elevator with a large bag. Kelly trailed behind her with another bag. Gunner and Adam jumped up to help them with their heavy load.

"What's in the bags?" DJ asked.

"These are the lead outfits," Kelly answered. "And since Mr. Gunner is the one with the image, my mom made several for him to try on."

"These are just for style, and whichever one you like can be made in any color."

"Well, give me the bags and I'll step into the "not quite working yet" restroom and try them on," Gunner said, responding with enthusiasm.

The eight kids and Kelly's mom each pulled up a chair and got settled for the fashion show about to take place.

After trying on several different styles and colors, Gunner came out with one that had a skirt, or Irish kilt, look. It was pink and blue and he was wearing tights underneath the skirt. When he stepped out in front of the kids, they all burst out laughing.

"How could this outfit protect us from the X rays?" Gunner asked, looking quite silly.

Kelly's mom could hardly stop laughing long enough to answer Mr. Gunner's question. "I'm sorry. That's a square-dancing outfit I made for my sister. It must have gotten mixed up in the pile."

A Fighting Chance

It was so hysterical to see him in that getup that they just couldn't stop laughing. Gunner even started laughing at himself and went back into the restroom to try on another outfit.

He came out dressed in a black jumpsuit. It had silver lightning bolts on the sleeves and the pant legs. All the kids gave a thumbs-up, and Yuri sighed with relief.

"You like it? Gunner asked as he modeled the outfit.

"It's perfect," Jackie remarked.

"I guess I should tell you now, Mr. Gunner, that it won't be necessary for you to wear one of these. The X rays are dangerous only to us back here at the work station."

"Well then," Gunner said in a jokingly disappointed tone of voice. "I'll just have to return to my dressing room, remove my Batman-looking outfit and deal with the fact that I, your fearless leader, will have to remain in civilian clothes."

"Oh brother," Jackie said.

"How do you think I feel," Dominique said. "I have to live with this all the time."

Everyone enjoyed laughing at the back and forth funny comments. Adam sat quietly with a smile on his face, enjoying the fact that he had friends and could be included in all the fun.

After his moment of enjoyment, Adam took charge again.

"I would like to suggest the colors of the outfits if

you will allow me, sir. DJ, Billy, Yuri, Jackie, Dominique and Josh, let's put you in blue because you will be the sector workers. Kelly, you should be in red so that I can find you when I'm looking around the room and I will be in yellow so all of you can pick me out should confusion hit, and at times it will. Does anyone have any objections to that?"

Surprisingly the entire group agreed and Kelly's mom left to get started making the outfits for everyone.

"Adam, you amaze me. Everything you say is well thought out and none of it is done with a selfish motive."

As Mr. Gunner said this, everyone got quiet. They took a moment to realize that the laboratory was finished and they had just seen Adam in action. They never knew this side of Adam, that this type of person actually went to their school. Everything Mr. Gunner just said was so true, and they all realized for the first time that they were proud to be friends with a person like Adam—a person they all used to make fun of.

Jackie realized that the mood was becoming too serious and broke the silence. "All right, enough with the *"we love Adam"* stuff. If his head gets any bigger, we're going to have dig him out of this basement."

"Yeah," DJ said jokingly. "Adam, do you think this stuff is really going to work?" he added.

"Pay attention and you'll see." Adam pointed to the center doors where Mr. Gunner would be.

"These doors stand about eight feet tall and are

made of steel." Adam continued to explain while he had everyone's full attention.

"This center door is called the 'C-1 Transport Door.' All entries and departures happen right from here. Anytime Mr. Gunner departs, we can watch everything he does on this six-foot screen."

The screen sat on top of the C-1 Transport Door. To the right and left of the transport door were sectors…three on each side.

"Each person will man a sector except Kelly. She will always remain on the mobile unit. Her work is vital to what I need to be doing next in a situation."

Near the three sectors on the right side of the transport was a large map.

"This map is the 'Joe Locator.' Sorry, Mr. Gunner, for calling you Joe. If we lose communications with you it will come up on the map as to your whereabouts. The good news is, with this little device we can never lose you. I'm sure that makes you happy, Dominique. This whole system is the nucleus of this laboratory. What can we call this? We need to give it a name for code communication."

"What about, 'The headquarters'?" Billy suggested.

"What about, 'The Underground Lab'?" Yuri giggled out.

"How about, 'The Transport Machine'?" Kelly said.

No one really liked any of the suggestions. From a chair just to the left of the main group was Josh. "The Zone," he said.

Everyone stopped thinking and looked toward Josh.

"I like it," Mr. Gunner said, giving it deeper thought.

The rest of the kids agreed. The more they said it to themselves, the more they liked the name.

"'The Zone' it is," Mr. Gunner said, finalizing the decision.

Adam tried to get back on track by explaining how The Zone worked.

"Anyway, this computer panel is the nucleus of The Zone. It is hooked into every satellite in space and is programmed to pick up any problem you can think of. You just target the state or area and a readout will be printed in minutes, if not sooner."

Adam opened a small box and handed each team member what looked like normal watches.

"This is how I can gather you together when a situation occurs. It looks like a watch, and it is. When I signal you to report to the lab, it will vibrate and beep at the same time. Displayed on the face of the watch will appear a number, 1, 2, or 3, depending on the seriousness of the case. Mr. Gunner, this is my pride and joy. Your watch is a little different. We will not call you until we have done our prep work. When we do call you, if you are too far away, you will press this button here on the side of the watch. This button will activate and immediately transport. A high-pitched wave will retrieve the field base transport unit and engage a transport door wherever you may be."

"Adam, that sounds great, but isn't this virtually impossible?" Gunner said, not wanting to crush Adam's creative ideas.

Adam replied, "Inconvenient? Yes. Impossible? No. Soon I will figure out how to transport without a base door. I didn't have time—I was a little busy this week. Anyway, who wants to give it a try?"

No one accepted. None of this seemed possible to any of them except Adam.

"I knew no one would volunteer, so I came prepared."

Adam went to a cage that he had brought earlier and reached for the three sleepy puppies inside.

"Adam, don't!" Kelly said with a merciful cry.

"Relax, there's nothing to worry about. Everybody, man your positions and put your hands on the keys."

"Mr. Gunner, you go upstairs and out behind the mill. Josh's idea of getting energy from the sun can fuel us more than we could ever use."

Gunner watched everyone move about and was very proud of how they were taking their jobs so seriously.

Adam picked up the puppies, gathering them in his arms. They were Cocker Spaniels.

"Okay, I hope these little guys don't turn into hotdogs," Gunner said jokingly in his zany voice.

"That is so dumb, Dad," Dominique responded as Gunner headed upstairs chuckling, knowing his goofy joke raised a few eyebrows.

Adam asked Billy to help him place the puppies into the C-1 Transport Door.

The boys were very gentle with the puppies. However, Kelly displayed a sad look, as if they wouldn't make it through this "mad scientist" experiment.

"You are worrying for nothing, Kelly," Adam said with confidence, knowing his work never failed. "The puppies are going to be fine. I would go myself if someone else knew how to work all this."

Billy placed the last puppy into the transport door

and remembered that they didn't have on the lead suits.

"Hey, what about the lead suits?"

"It's okay," Adam said. "One time won't hurt."

Adam hit a switch on the control panel next to Josh and it closed the C-1 Transport Door. Kelly grabbed tightly onto the rail, still not convinced this would work.

Every person stood intently at their individual control stations with their hands on the keys, waiting for instructions from Adam.

"All right, I'm beginning the countdown: Five... four... three... two... one... now!"

All the keys turned at once.

"Begin transporting," Adam said with a firm look on his face.

Kelly grabbed the rail tighter and let out a little squeal. Everyone was so caught up in the moment that they didn't even respond to Kelly's concerned outburst. There was a massive rumbling sound accompanied by a bright light, which came from inside the C-1 Transport Door.

Dominique noticed a red light that had appeared on her control panel. "Adam, what does this red light mean?"

"Good! It works!" Adam replied. "Decrease power in sectors two and five by 3 percent."

Dominique knew exactly what to do and quickly responded to Adam's order.

Standing outside in back of the mill, Gunner

waited for something—anything. He wasn't sure what was going to happen, but he was willing to go along with what Adam had asked him to do.

After a moment, Gunner not only heard but also felt a rumbling. Within moments the ground began to wave like water and out of the ground came a door similar to the transport that was inside. It came out from the ground and locked into position. There was absolutely no expression on Gunner's face. He couldn't believe what he was seeing! He came to the conclusion that there was no technology like this anywhere on earth. Shaking his head to make sure all of this was truly happening, he moved closer to the door. It quickly opened and a small amount of smoke or fog dispersed out. Gunner stepped inside the doors and there were the three puppies, safe and sound.

A Fighting Chance

"Oh my gosh! It really worked. I can't believe it really worked!" he said, dumbfounded. Gunner didn't reach for the puppies or move at all. The rest of the kids came piling out of the mill at top speed toward the transport door. Kelly was the first one there. She took a look at the safe puppies and clasped her hands over her mouth.

Billy gave Adam a high five.

"Satisfied, Kelly?" Adam asked with confidence.

"I can't believe it really worked!" she responded. "I've never heard of anything like this before."

"That's because there is nothing like this," Adam replied as he continued. "It's only the beginning. What we did in the classroom is nothing compared to what we are going to be able to do now."

Chapter 19

Things Are About to Heat up Back at School

Mr. Gunner got out of his car, all dressed in his same crazy outfit as usual. He walked over to the front entrance and saw a baseball rolling toward him. Two kids were playing catch before the morning bell and the ball got away from them.

Being a good sport, Gunner picked up the ball and heaved it to the kid closest to him. Of course, Gunner's aim was so far off that it beelined straight at Miss Ward's office window. Having no mercy on Gunner, the ball crashed through the window and glass flew everywhere.

The kids took off running and Gunner picked up his pace, hoping he could get in the building before he was caught. Unfortunately, it wasn't going to work out as he had hoped. Just as the bell rang, Miss Ward came running out of the school with the baseball in her hand.

A Fighting Chance

She didn't even look around to see who threw it. She spotted Gunner and motioned her with her finger for him to come. Gunner froze in his tracks, then walked in his goofy way toward the angry Miss Ward.

The closer Gunner got to Miss Ward, the more she realized she was asking for more trouble if she came in contact with Gunner.

"What am I doing?" she asked herself. "I can't even have a simple conversation with this man without him destroying half of my office."

She instantly put up her hand, motioning for Gunner to stop walking toward her, which he did.

"Don't come any closer," the aggravated Miss Ward said. "I'm going back into the school. Don't move until I am safely inside my office with my door locked. Is that clear, Mr. Gunner?"

"Absolutely, Miss Ward. You could say it's like a little game of freeze tag."

She let out a disgusted sigh and quickly walked back into the building. Gunner watched her storm off.

"I didn't win any points with her on that comment. Funny thing is, the ball really did slip out of my hand," he said to himself in his normal voice.

Gunner didn't realize that at that same time, Rodney's car was leaving the other side of the parking lot. The car pulled out of sight and Ryles made his way toward Gunner.

Mr. Gunner kept his frozen stance in obedience to Miss Ward's stern request. Gunner figured he had waited long enough and it was safe to enter the building. But he didn't see Ryles, who was running toward him. Gunner barely took a step when Ryles called out for him to wait up. Turning around and in character, Gunner waited for him to get there.

Arriving out of breath, Ryles put his hands on his knees and took a moment to catch his breath and calm down.

"I'm scared, Mr. Gunner. Rodney originally told me two or three weeks. I don't remember exactly, but he said to forget it now. He wants me to make a decision tonight! I don't know what he might do to me!"

"Do you know what your problem is, son? You worry too much. Worry not. When a problem like this occurs, you alert the proper authorities, as you have just done, and they will tell you what to do. I'll make sure you are safe. Now where does he want to meet you?"

"By the fence at the back of the school grounds fifteen minutes after school lets out."

"Ryles, enjoy your day and don't worry about a thing. The proper authorities will be there. You won't know who they are, but they'll be there. Okay?"

Ryles nodded with some uncertainty. Gunner put his arm around Ryles to comfort him as they both walked into the school. Once they were in the school, Ryles went one way and Gunner went another.

Miss Ward stepped out of her office and called out to Gunner, motioning that she would like to speak with him.

A Fighting Chance

Gunner didn't realize that Miss Ward had been watching him from her window. Miss Ward displayed a stern look on her face and had her hands on her hips. Gunner could tell she wasn't happy.

"Good morning, Miss Ward. I take it you're having a good one, I hope."

"Mr. Gunner, since you have been here at our school, you have destroyed our scoreboard, broken my window and made a mess in my office. I still believe you had something to do with the fiasco in the hallway the other day, not to mention I told you not to go near my nephew, and you went against my word!"

"I—" Gunner tried to get out of it, but Miss Ward kept going.

"None of that bothers me. Do you know why? Please don't answer. The school board called and today is your last day. They've granted me another replacement. Do you know how happy that makes me, Mr. Gunner?"

"Extremely?" he replied.

"That's the first thing you've said right since you've been here."

"Well, that's great. I'm happy for you. I mean, whatever makes you happy, Miss Ward. That's what I want to see for you. You are a good principal and I'll miss you."

Gunner began tearily expressing that he would miss her. She didn't know he was faking, but she was at her wit's end with him and would not let this emotion get to her.

"Oh, moments like this are touching," Gunner said as he continued. "I never like good-byes. I'd better just get going to my class. Oh, I'll miss you all."

Gunner extended his hand to her and she responded with a handshake. She really didn't know how to respond to him, so she got the handshake over with and walked off.

As soon as she left, Gunner stopped the sniffles and continued on his way. He had more serious things to worry about and needed to get away from her as soon as possible.

Later That Day

The school day passed, and Gunner was in his last study hall class with The Fighting Chance Team. He walked around the classroom giving instructions.

"This is it. It's all about to go down and you know that it's not a game."

They listened intently as Mr. Gunner spoke in his normal voice. He spoke sternly so that their safety would be secure.

"Do exactly what I say. If any of you attempt to be a hero, our work together is through. Do I make myself clear?"

They all acknowledged his request. "I am the front

line guy. You are the office control managers. As soon as school gets out, you have fifteen minutes to get to the mill, set up and get ready. Adam, hook up all video and audio communication and insert a tape in the recorder. We might need it."

"Yes, sir." Adam replied with respect.

"I'll need the phone communicator and, Adam, I'll need you to place the video camera in my bow tie. Does anyone have any questions? If not, then let's get to work."

The kids could see that Adam had no questions, therefore they didn't have any either. They were prepared to respond to whatever Adam needed to make this all work.

Gunner removed his bow tie and Adam went to work on it. It took only a moment to insert the pea-sized video camera. He gave it back to Gunner, who placed it back around his neck.

The bell rang and the kids were off.

Gunner waited five minutes and then made his way into the hall. He wanted to avoid any contact that could slow him down or get in his way. He saw Mr. Edwards heading right toward him. Gunner figured that he had come this far and now was not the time to let the cat out of the bag.

Gunner got back into character and looked up to receive the oncoming Mr. Edwards.

"I understand this is your last day, Mr. Gunner."

"Yes, it is, and let me add that it was a pleasure

working with you. You're a wonderful physical education teacher. I'm sorry to be leaving."

Gunner quickly walked off.

"I'm not," Mr. Edwards said under his breath.

Gunner made his way out the school's front doors, and, much to his surprise, Ryles was walking toward Rodney. Gunner quickly looked down at his watch.

"Oh no! They're early."

He reached for his phone communicator and pushed a few buttons.

He began to speak in his normal voice. "This is Detective Galardi. I'll need back-up to stand by. On my signal, have them meet me at Metro Middle School. Over."

Gunner didn't wait for a response. He had done this many times and had great faith in his dispatch squad. As soon as he hung up his phone, he contacted Adam via his watch.

"Adam, it's going to go down right now. Alert the team and get to The Zone immediately."

"I'm already here. We're waiting on Josh. Mr. Gunner, this isn't good. My satellite receptors are showing hot spots in different locations around the school."

"What?" Gunner asked with great concern.

"Rodney has his boys everywhere. I've got eight on radar. What do you want me to do? By the way, Josh is here now. We're ready to go."

"Give me a minute to think," Gunner said.

"Too late, they're in the building," Adam said.

"Where? Give me exact locations."

Adam's level of intensity went up as he answered.

"Umm...Two in Miss Ward's office. Four are moving in and out of the computer room...ah...two are at the back fence."

"They're robbing the school," Gunner said.

"Wait, wait," Adam added. "There are three other bodies in Miss Ward's office. Total of five now."

"Listen closely. They're holding people hostage. Adam, stay with me. Follow me and tell me what is going on around me at all times."

"Yes, sir," Adam replied, knowing he must stay calm to make this work.

Gunner spoke into his phone communicater. "I need back-up ASAP. Do not come in advertising, though. Stay low. Over."

Back in the main office, Miss Ward, Mr. Edwards and Mrs. Rossenheimer were being held hostage at gunpoint.

They were all so scared that Mrs. Rossenheimer was almost to the point of fainting.

"Take whatever you want, but don't hurt us," Miss Ward said with fear in her voice.

The thug who was holding her at gunpoint responded, "We will take whatever we want. If you don't want to get hurt, you need to lower the volume. You got it, sister?"

Miss Ward didn't even answer. She just nodded as

a tear rolled down her face.

The door opened suddenly and in walked the nerdy Mr. Gunner. He was carrying a note pad, so he really wasn't looking up when he entered. He was in full character, but he knew exactly what he was doing. With his head still down, he began to speak.

"Excuse me, Miss Ward, would you happen—," He cut himself off as he looked up to see that there was a room full of people.

"Oh, I didn't know you had company. Excuse me, gentlemen. I didn't mean to interrupt."

The thug with the gun then pointed it in Gunner's direction.

"You're at the wrong place at the wrong time, Nerd Man."

"Oh, I'll just be leaving then. I'll get back with you all later, okay? Have a great day."

Gunner acted in full denial that there was a hostage crisis going on. He turned and headed toward the door. He stopped when the thug with the gun put it in his back.

"I don't think so," the thug said. "You need to stick around for a while."

The thug had done exactly what Gunner wanted him to do. With the gun pressed up against his back, Gunner could defend himself the way he needed to.

"You know, that is a very dangerous piece of material you're holding in your hand. You should consider placing that back in its proper holster,"

A Fighting Chance

Gunner said in his zany voice.

Mr. Edwards closed his eyes in disgust. He realized Gunner was in real trouble.

"Hey!" the thug shouted, trying to get Gunner to shut up.

The loud shout gave Gunner the opportunity to act scared. However, knowing exactly what he was doing, Gunner turned in his nerdy way and used a clumsy elbow move to knock the gun out of the thug's hand. Gunner used his tactics of goofiness and fell on the thug who had the gun. As they fell to the ground, Gunner discreetly pushed the thug's head into the ground, knocking him unconscious.

Gunner stood to his feet and looked at the second thug. "I didn't mean to fall."

The second thug grabbed Gunner by the shirt and tried to manhandle him. Gunner used his body weight to throw the second thug off guard. Gunner flung the second thug into the bookshelves. Gunner acted like he tripped and threw himself into the bookshelves as well, causing all the shelves to fall on top of the second thug. Without anyone seeing, Gunner took a book and hit the second thug on the head, knocking him unconscious.

Regaining composure, Gunner acted surprised. "Well, would you look at that? I'll tell you something. Those two karate classes were worth every bit of what I paid."

Mr. Gunner heard Adam through his earpiece. No

one else could hear Adam's voice, so Gunner could not give any facial responses that might reveal that Adam was talking to him.

"Mr. Gunner, officers are reeling in the four thugs who were in the computer room. I'll send two your way. Actually, just open your door. They are passing by right now."

Gunner opened the door and spotted two uniformed officers right in front of the door. "Isn't that something?" he said to Mr. Edwards, Miss Ward and Mrs. Rossenheimer, who were still in shock that guns had been pointed at them.

"Oh boys, could I borrow your services in here, please? You see, you can always count on the law enforcement when you need them. If you'll excuse me…,".

Gunner left the office, and the officers didn't even recognize him because he was still very much in character.

The officers cuffed the thugs and began to read them their rights.

Out in back of the school, Ryles made his way with confidence toward Rodney and his bodyguard friend. Ryles didn't fear the situation because Mr. Gunner had said that everything would be all right.

As they met, Rodney gave Ryles a weak handshake. "Today's the day, man. What do you have to say for yourself?" Rodney asked Ryles with a very cocky, controlling attitude.

A Fighting Chance

"I don't know," Ryles answered.

The bodyguard took a step toward Ryles, trying to intimidate him. "You heard the man. He's waiting for an answer."

"It's no!" Ryles said with authority.

"I don't think I heard you," Rodney said, giving him another chance to give him the answer he wanted.

Ryles was not going to back down. "I said, 'No'. My friends and I are finished, and if you were smart, you'd get out, too."

The two started laughing at Ryles's comment.

Gunner was heading toward them, while at a distance behind Gunner, Miss Ward was on her way as well. She was told that her nephew was being harassed in the lot in the back of the school. She was not aware that the boys harassing Ryles were connected with the two who were in her office earlier. She thought that they were students from the school.

Adam relayed a message to Mr. Gunner through the earpiece. "All are in custody except the two you are going after. Rodney is on parole. This is going to do him in, Mr. Gunner."

"Thanks, Adam. Stay with me."

Gunner slowed down his approach so he could get a grasp on what was going on and to try to figure out how to handle this situation.

By then, Rodney was acting very cocky toward Ryles and started getting a little rough with him, trying to intimidate him.

Rodney felt the sleeves on Ryles's shirt, insinuating that some of the money he gave Ryles could have paid for the shirt.

"I believe I might have paid for this shirt," Rodney said as he ripped the sleeves. "I want it back."

That sent fear through Ryles. Rodney was about twenty years old and Ryles was only in middle school.

Gunner finally arrived on the scene and a lot of kids were gathering around at a distance from them.

The Fighting Chance Team was completely aware of everything that was going on and realized that this was the crucial point in the mission. They were all ready and remained alert.

"Adam, we have audio and video," Kelly said.

"Keep an eye on the satellite scope. Watch for people coming behind him," Adam said as he continued. "Josh, activate the tape recorder."

"Activated," Josh replied.

Gunner approached the threesome in complete character. "What is it you boys need to talk to one of my students about?"

"You'd best leave now, Nerd Man," Rodney said with authority.

Gunner realized that everything was about to come loose, but he couldn't back down, and he couldn't expose who he was, so he stayed in character and tried to respond with authority.

"I believe you boys have it the other way around. I'm sure of it. You'd best leave! This is school property and violent behavior is not acceptable at any time."

Adam warned Mr. Gunner through the earpiece. "Mr. Gunner, both guys are carrying guns. Also, Rodney and the blonde goon each have over three ounces of cocaine on them."

Rodney pulled out a knife and grabbed Mr. Gunner by the collar. He put the knife to Gunner's throat.

Back at The Zone, they could see everything that was going on. The satellite scope that was in Mr. Gunner's bow tie bounced off the satellite, giving a 360-degree view of the present situation. Dominique screamed when she saw the knife at her father's throat. Adam tried to calm her down.

Meanwhile, back on the school grounds, Miss Ward had joined the large group of spectators and she was stunned to see Mr. Gunner with a knife to his throat.

Gunner didn't move. He knew there would be an opportunity to defend himself, but just then was not the right time.

"If you don't want me to cut this nerd man, I suggest you stay right where you are," Rodney said to Miss Ward.

"You know, you boys are in a lot of trouble," Gunner said in total zany character.

Adam gave Mr. Gunner a reminder about the cocaine in Rodney's right pocket.

"Do you realize how much jail time you are going to do when they find out that you have over three ounces of cocaine in your right pocket?" Gunner said, responding to Adam's information.

Rodney was startled, not knowing how this guy knew that.

"How did you know that?" Rodney said,

continuing to threaten Gunner. "You breathe a word of this and you're dead. You hear me, Nerd Man?"

"I've had about enough of this disrespectful kind of talking," Gunner said. "I'm going to give you to the count of three, and if you don't let me go, I'm going to karate the both of you."

That comment brought arrogant chuckles from Rodney and his goon bodyguard.

Miss Ward put her hands to her face and shook her head at that last comment.

He's going to get himself killed, Miss Ward said to herself, fearing for Mr. Gunner's life.

Gunner began the countdown: "Three…"

Adam and the team were watching everything back at The Zone.

"This guy doesn't know what's about to happen to him. He'd better let go," Adam said, knowing that Mr. Gunner was about to hurt him badly.

"Two…" Gunner said, as he continued his countdown. "I'm not kidding. I will karate the both of you if you don't let me go."

"I can hardly wait," Rodney said, completely unconcerned about Gunner's countdown. "Grab the kid and let's go," Rodney said to his bodyguard.

"One!"

On one, Gunner reached for the bodyguard's hand that was grabbing Ryles and twisted it. He used the bodyguard's arm to knock the knife out of Rodney's hand. The bodyguard swung at Gunner's head, but

Gunner slipped out of the way and the bodyguard smacked Rodney squarely in the jaw, sending him to the ground. Gunner twisted the bodyguard's arm and threw him on top of Rodney.

Gunner was not acting in his goofy character, but was defending himself and the innocent people standing around him.

Miss Ward was more in shock at what she saw Gunner doing than what was happening with the whole situation.

With both guys on the ground, one on top of the other, Gunner pulled out handcuffs and cuffed them both.

It was hard for everyone watching to take what just happened seriously because Mr. Gunner still looked like his zany character.

A Fighting Chance

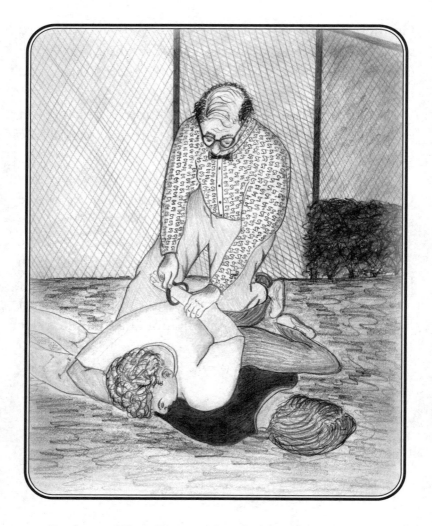

Back at The Zone, the kids were going crazy because they had never seen Mr. Gunner in action before.

"Man, did you see that?" Yuri said giggling.

"He didn't even throw one punch," DJ said in total amazement.

"That's my dad," Dominique said with a sigh of relief.

But it wasn't over yet. While the others were in awe, Adam was still very serious and in work mode.

"Mr. Gunner, I'm alerting backup to your location. Over."

Back on the field, Mr. Gunner had his knee in the back of the bodyguard as he lay face down on top of Rodney.

"Well done, Adam," Gunner said aloud, still in his zany voice.

The sirens were now coming in loud and clear and the backup was in visual sight.

Miss Ward, Mrs. Rossenheimer and Mr. Edwards were very confused about what just happened. There must have been seventy or more students from the school gathered around all of the activity.

Gunner looked around at all the people. He was about to reveal who he really was. He started by taking off his glasses and then followed by removing the funny-looking teeth he was wearing over his real teeth. He paused for a moment and then removed the bald wig, exposing his own full head of hair.

A Fighting Chance

The students were all in shock as they murmured amongst themselves. Miss Ward, Mrs. Rossenheimer and Mr. Edwards stood dumbfounded, not knowing what to say or do. The police arrived at the scene and the officers from inside the building were walking the two handcuffed kids they had arrested to the police car.

With everyone still in shock after Gunner's unveiling, Joseph Galardi, known to them as Mr. Gunner, began to read Rodney and his bodyguard their rights. This was another shock. This was the first time they had heard his real voice.

"You have the right to remain silent. You have the right to an attorney. Anything you say can and will be used against you in a court of law. If you can't provide an attorney, the court will appoint one for you."

One of the officers from the police cars grabbed the two boys Gunner was holding.

"Good job, Galardi. We'll take it from here," the officer said, bringing both boys to their feet.

"You'll find a nice gift in their pockets," Gunner said, referring to the three ounces of cocaine.

The officers reached in the boys' pockets and pulled out exactly what Gunner said would be there. Those two thieves knew they were going to jail for a long time.

They both looked at Gunner and gave him a dirty look.

"I told you I was going to karate you guys," Gunner said in his zany voice just to be funny.

The officers took all the criminals away.

Ryles, who hadn't said a word the whole time, was in shock. He walked over and gave Gunner a big hug, knowing that Gunner had just saved his life. Miss Ward made her way toward her nephew. When she got close to him, he let go of Gunner and hugged his aunt. She comforted him with a hug in return and slowly looked up at Mr. Gunner.

"I'm sorry. I don't know what to say," Miss Ward said as tears began to stream down her face.

"You don't have to say anything. Your nephew is going to be fine. He's a good boy and he knows how to make the right decisions." Gunner spoke to Ryles saying, "Now you can see how one bad decision can make a lot of trouble for a lot of innocent people."

Back at The Zone, the kids were cheering and excited that they had been a part of what just happened.

"I feel like we were a bunch of doctors who just delivered quadruplets in the elevator of a high-rise building," DJ said with a sigh of relief that it was all over.

"You guys did a great job. We all did," Adam said. "I'm proud to call you all my friends."

"We're going to be friends for a long time," Josh said unexpectedly.

"Count me in on that," Jackie said.

"Me too," Billy said.

"Me three," Yuri giggled.

"We're all in," Kelly added.

"All right, enough of the mushy stuff. I gotta go. I'll see you guys at school tomorrow," DJ reported.

"We don't have school tomorrow. It's Saturday," Dominique commented cheerfully.

"Go ahead. You can all leave. I'll come in tomorrow and clean up," Adam said.

"No, we'll all help you," Kelly said, fully intending to work.

"Okay, let's all come in for an hour or so and clean up," Adam suggested.

They all agreed they would meet the next day before lunch to clean up The Zone.

Chapter 20

The Day After

I t was a beautiful Saturday morning. The sun was out, and birds were singing. School was not in session, but the superintendent had called a meeting because there was a lot of paperwork that needed to be filled out due to Friday's incident.

Miss Ward, Mrs. Rossenheimer and Mr. Edwards, along with the superintendent were all in Miss Ward's office when there was a knock at the door. The superintendent answered the door, and in walked Joseph Galardi, A.K.A. Joseph Gunner. He was very well-dressed, all cleaned up and looking real good.

The two ladies were shocked, especially Miss Ward, who had had many encounters with Mr. Gunner in this very office, each ending in destruction.

Gunner was aware that they all felt uncomfortable because of how they had treated him, so he addressed them politely, like a gentleman.

"Good afternoon, ladies and Mr. Edwards. My name is Joseph Galardi. I am a detective for the Metro area. I am also Dominique and Nicole's dad. If you want to know why you couldn't get a replacement for me, it was because your superintendent, Mr. Baxter, was working with me on this case."

No one knew what to say. They were stunned. Miss Ward just laughed as she rewound the past days in her head.

Then everyone was silent, and Joseph continued. "I've never been to school on a Saturday before."

Miss Ward gathered her composure and spoke from her heart. "I don't know what to say. I judged you wrongly, and I could have lost my nephew because of it. I learned as much of a lesson as Ryles did."

"Here," Joseph said, as he handed a check to Miss Ward. "This should cover all the damages from my stay."

"I don't think that will be necessary, Mr. Galardi," the superintendent said.

"It's part of the job. Take it, please," replied Joseph.

Miss Ward took the envelope and Joseph extended his hand to Miss Ward, then to Mrs. Rossenheimer, and finally to Mr. Edwards.

Miss Ward was fighting back the tears. This was very emotional for her. "Thank you so much. Again, I'm sorry," she said.

"Don't be sorry. We got the bad guys and, at the same time, kept a couple of good kids from going bad. How can you beat that?"

Without warning, Joseph's watch went off and scared the daylights out of him. They looked at him, not knowing what was wrong.

Joseph realized that no one must ever find out about The Fighting Chance Team or The Zone. If they did, it would get into the press and everything would be ruined in a matter of time.

"Whoa! Sorry about that. Still trying to get used to this new watch. Gotta go."

Joseph Galardi left the office and quickly made his way out the front door of the school. As soon as he got outside, he answered the page from his watch.

"I copy you, Control Central. What's the emergency?" Galardi asked.

While waiting for Adam to respond, Joseph climbed aboard his Harley. Adam's voice came through the watch loud and clear.

"Detective Galardi," Adam said.

"Just call me Mr. Galardi, Adam. The job is over."

"Okay, Mr. Galardi. All of us are here at the mill cleaning up The Zone and the satellite has picked up a very interesting situation. I don't think you will want to miss it. It's a big one. If you don't get there fast it's going to be too late. You want to try the transport?"

Joseph didn't even take a moment to think about it. "Yes, I do."

A Fighting Chance

"Hit the retrieve button. When the door comes up out of the ground, you and the bike get in and hit the send button on your watch. We'll take it from there. The job's not over, Mr. Galardi. It's just beginning."

Mr. Galardi hit the button as Adam instructed. There was a loud noise. The door came up, and Mr. Galardi pulled the bike in. He pushed the send button, and the door closed. There was a loud explosion with lightning bolts flashing around the door. The ground began to ripple and, in an instant, the door was gone!

Back at The Zone, the team had taken their positions and were following Adam's command to accomplish this first transfer.

"Modulation overload, Adam. What should I do?" Kelly asked.

"Why is this happening? There should be no overload," Adam said with great concern as he continued. "Josh, give me a readout on your screen."

"No readout as of yet," Josh replied.

"Kelly, do you have a time and point of arrival yet?" Adam asked with greater concern.

The red light started to flash, and the alarm began to sound. Everyone moved frantically at their workstations, giving Adam every readout he asked for.

Another alarm sounded, and then two went off at the same time. Adam quickly moved to the large map that had been titled the "Joe Locator."

Adam quickly tried to pinpoint Mr. Galardi's whereabouts when both alarms suddenly stopped. The entire team froze. Everyone stared at Adam, but he didn't move a muscle. There was silence, and a coldness filled the room.

Dominique broke the silence; "Adam, where's my dad?"

He slowly turned his head toward Dominique and answered very quietly, "I don't know."

I would like to take this time to say thank you to my 4th grade teacher, Mrs. Christine Wilkes. She is a very dear lady who made an impact on my life very early on. She encouraged me, inspired me and always desired to see all her students succeed.

The wonderful seeds she planted will continue for many years to come.

Christine Wilkes is still teaching, encouraging and inspiring students today.

Thank you, Mrs. Wilkes.

—Joe Manno

About the Illustrator

Cynthia Woodhouse, illustrator of *A Fighting Chance*, has been drawing and creating things with her hands since her childhood. After illustrating covers for high school newspapers, the field of stage captured her attention in college, leading Cynthia to create special effects stage make-up, design production posters, and work on set designs. She has a B.A. in Fine Arts from Mount Vernon Nazarene College. Since college, Cynthia's work has been presented in art shows, church worship art, various logo designs and has been seen in *New Man* magazine. Her interest in art therapy led her to a partnership with another community artist on a student tile wall project at a local middle school to help kids cope with a fatal gun shot tragedy in the school. Cynthia is currently active in a community artist group and relaxes with painting, card design, still photography, and mixed media.

Who is RTC Entertainment, Inc.?

RTC Entertainment's mission is to reach the children and youth with positive messages of life utilizing the entertainment industry as its primary vehicle.

RTC Entertainment, Inc. is a not-for-profit 501 (c) (3) company located in Orlando, Florida dedicated to reaching the children with positive messages and realistic solutions to issues faced by today's youth. RTC Entertainment, Inc. was co-founded by and remains under the leadership of Joseph D. Manno and Anthony DeRosa.

We look forward to hearing from you.

RTC ENTERTAINMENT INC
REACHING THE CHILDREN
P . O . B O X 6 0 9 1 3 8
ORLANDO, FLORIDA 32860-9138
www.rtcentertainment.com

Look for Book 2 as the journey continues.

Dear Friend,

Thank you for reading my book. I hope you enjoyed the story.

Just as the characters in this book, you, too, are unique. You, too, can make a difference in this world. You are important. There is no one like you anywhere on the face of this earth. You are one of a kind. You have to go after your dreams, believe in yourself, and never give up! You are a leader!

Don't believe any lies that people might tell you that make you feel bad about yourself. You are special, you are needed, and the future depends on you.

Your friend,

Joe Manno

For more information on Joe Manno,
check out the website at

www.rtcentertainment.com